Free To Believe

Free To Believe

Ten Steps to Faith

MICHAEL PAUL GALLAGHER SJ

Foreword by Jean Vanier

Darton, Longman and Todd
London

First published in 1987 by
Darton, Longman and Todd Ltd
89 Lillie Road, London SW6 1UD

© 1987 Michael Paul Gallagher SJ

ISBN 0 232 51723 1

British Library Cataloguing in Publication Data

Gallagher, Michael Paul
   Free to believe: ten steps to faith.
   1. Christian life
   I. Title
   248.4   BV4501.2

ISBN 0–232–51723–1

Phototypeset by Input Typesetting Ltd, London SW19 8DR
Printed and bound by Anchor Brendon Ltd, Tiptree, Essex

Contents

Foreword

Michael Paul Gallagher's book is about a journey in three parts: opening the doors of a prison, starting out on a quest and finishing in an encounter. This encounter is a moment of trust and communion which brings meaning and which, as he says, leads to 'the battle zone of pride and poverty where Jesus fights for our full freedom and remains dissatisfied with a half-freedom'.

Free To Believe helps us to understand this 'battle zone' where each one of us is called to struggle and to receive this freedom to love as Jesus loves. In my own 'battle zone', the community of l'Arche where I have been living for over twenty years with men and women who have a mental handicap, we work together, share our meals together, pray together, have fun, and sometimes even fight with each other. And together we are learning how to forgive each other. I am struck by the way in which so many of those we have welcomed seem deeply imprisoned in strange, unreal dreams, in anger, depression or in their broken psyche. They are closed in upon themselves. But deeper than these prisons I have discovered a cry, a quest, a yearning for love, for meaning and for recognition. Some of the men and women with whom we live have accepted their situation because they have been accepted by someone else. They have discovered that they are loved just as they are, and this love has led them to another love, an experience of Jesus which has brought them a new fulfilment, a deeper peace, a form of wholeness. Their eyes are no longer dulled with pain, anger, depression and self-centredness. A light is shining there.

Michael Paul Gallagher is a priest of Jesus. This book is obviously not born out of books, theories and ideas but out of his many personal experiences with people whom he has accompanied on their journey. He has listened to them as a priest and has heard in their hearts and in their questions the yearning to escape from the prison, to advance on the quest of life and then to meet that person who is the source of life and who gives us freedom.

Can I ask you to read this book quietly and gently? Through the journey Michael Paul Gallagher describes, you will recognize the stages of your own life, you will be able to re-read your own journey. At the beginning and at the end of this journey there is a person, a gentle lover, yearning to take from your shoulders the yoke of guilt and to lead you to a new and greater freedom and fullness of love.

JEAN VANIER
l'Arche, Trosly-Breuil
France

January 1987

Io veggio ben che giammai non si sazia
  Nostro intelletto, se il ver non lo illustra,
  Di fuor dal qual nessun vero si spazia.

Posasi in esso, come fiera in lustra,
  Tosto che giunto l'ha: e giugner puollo
  Se non, ciascun disio sabebbe frustra.

Nasce per quello, a guisa di rampollo.
  Appie del vero il dubbio: ed e natura,
  Ch'al summo pinge noi de collo in collo.
                    Dante, *Paradiso*, IV, 124–32

I see it well: my mind will never be at peace,
till that Truth dawn upon it which hides
no further truth beyond itself.

Arriving there the mind will rest at last
like a wild beast at home within its lair;
and that arrival must be possible, unless
desire is doomed to mere frustration.

Meanwhile doubt upon doubt arise,
like off-shoots from the foot of truth;
it is our nature that such questions spur us
from hill to hill onward towards the summit.

Introduction: Three Kinds of Stories

I can only answer the question 'What am I to do?' if I can answer the prior question 'Of what story or stories do I find myself a part?'
Alasdair MacIntyre

This will be a book about faith, but first of all it is about bothering to be free. Why put it that way? Because most people, myself included, do not always bother to be free, and because most of our difficulties over faith are linked with this lack of freedom. Seldom are they a problem of truth on its own.

Personally, when I run into a bout of doubt, there is nearly always an unfreedom to be found. I may have fallen into some kind of superficial living – being over-busy and yet spiritually under-nourished. It may be that my human faith – my trust in others or in myself – has been dented through some hurt or disappointment. Or I could be drifting with the tides around me, in which case the prevailing currents make God unreal. Whatever the source, there are moments when faith in God becomes eclipsed, literally, because something has got in the way. When that happens there is no point exploring the meaning of faith while forgetting the unfree self, just as it is futile to tinker with the television set if the power fuse has blown. I have to go to where the trouble lies, and this will mean some struggle to escape.

During my childhood I was fascinated by escape stories, and in that period after the Second World War there seemed an endless supply of them. Many years after I had outgrown my addiction to such stories, it came home to me that there was a religious parallel there. Christian faith is not a matter of believing historical or invisible facts. It has much more to do with stories, true stories, escape stories. Right from the foundation event of the Jewish faith, called Exodus, to the foundation event of Christian faith, called Resurrection, it is escape stories all the way.

ESCAPING FROM PRISON

Those prison escapes of my childhood reading seem to have had a basic plot in common; at least that is the way I now remember them. There was usually a first period when the prisoners had to become convinced that freedom was possible and when they had to summon up the will to escape. Someone with imagination would awaken the hopes of the others. Often there was one important prisoner who initially showed no interest in trying to escape, because he had settled into prison life and become apathetic. So the first stage of the escape story would involve a drama of motivation, a struggle of dispositions and attitudes. Once people saw that freedom was not impossible, there followed a secretly active period of preparing the escape, assembling the equipment, digging a tunnel, rehearsing the various roles.

Eventually came the adventure of the escape itself: in addition to the predictable enemies of dogs, search-lights, barbed wire, electrified fences, gun turrets and so on, nearly always something unforeseen happened to heighten the drama. The battery of a carefully concealed torch is found to have gone damp. Wirecutters are left behind and someone has to return to the hut. A friendly guard comes in for a chat just as everything is about to go into operation. But these setbacks are somehow overcome. The prisoners scale the final obstacle and are 'away'. But the drama was not yet over because they were still within enemy territory and a long journey remained before full freedom. As well as all the outer dangers of the road, the new enemy is despair: the escapees need one another's encouragement to keep going, and few escapees managed to travel through enemy territory without some help, either planned or fortunately found along the way.

In these pages I want to explore faith as, at least initially, an escape story. Without some self-liberation, on various levels, faith can be impossible today. But this freedom is only a first, even if difficult, adventure. Many questions remain: why are we here at all? is God just a fantasy? what am I looking for in life? if God exists, can I somehow experience him? and what difference would faith make anyway? After our first part, entitled 'Escape Stories', a second part of this book is called 'Quest Stories': it moves on to questions like these, and in particular it explores four major ways of searching for God.

But searching does not necessarily imply finding, or that there is Anyone to be found. Another route remains. Our third section is called 'Love Stories', and it is here that Jesus Christ enters the picture. For everyone who becomes a Christian the pivot is the discovery of God through this Man. For some people that relationship is the beginning and end of the journey. But my hunch is that for many of my 'unbelieving' friends any possible revelation has to be prepared. Escape stories and quest stories naturally come first; only then do the love stories become credible.

A TRIPLE PATTERN

I have noticed this pattern unfold in many areas, from the questionings of others to my own prayer. Over my eighteen years in university teaching, I have greatly enjoyed spending time with students who wanted to talk about 'religion'. But as long as we were discussing faith as a problem 'out there', the conversation remained at a distance from personal reality. It lacked bite, because for most of the students I have known the real struggles were not primarily religious. So over the years I found myself drawn to change the agenda of such meetings. I would surprise people by saying, 'I'm not interested in talking about God; I'm more interested in talking about you'. At first this was rooted in a hunch that what they wanted was not God-talk but a space for self-truth. Gradually this became a deliberate approach, and as such it is the basis of this book. Some 'struggle to escape' from a superficially argumentative self may be needed before the deep quests and questions can be broached. And perhaps it is only after this slow slog of searching that one can reach the threshold of Revelation – which is God's love story.

I see much the same rhythm in my own efforts to pray. Nearly always I begin from scatteredness and it takes patience to 'escape' imprisonment in small distractions and to gather myself into some unity and quiet. Only then can I enter a stage of reaching out for God – another version of 'quest'. Sometimes I can eventually experience a grace of listening to 'love' and of being strengthened for loving. This book hopes to study that sequence of three stories as a natural set of roads to faith. Perhaps it is only after I have battled through to initial self-freedom, and only after I have struggled with many questions, that I will be ripe for the encounter with Christ.

Our plan, then, is to explore the struggle for faith as a triple journey or a triple story:

a journey of freedom – escape stories;
a journey of truth – quest stories;
a journey of receiving and giving – love stories.

Those three movements will correspond to the three parts of this book. And it is a pattern that may recur many times within one life-story: after escaping and questing, we are more ready for love.

As well as this development of the book through three main movements, it can also be read, as the subtitle suggests, as a series of ten steps towards faith. Four steps concern various kinds of freedom (escape stories). Four steps explore different approaches to the question of God (quest stories). Two final steps move into the fundamentals of Christian revelation (love stories). The quest and love themes will be touched upon further at the beginning of their respective sections.

OUR FOCUS HERE

For whom are these pages intended? My previous book, *Help my Unbelief* seems to have been of interest to two different groups of readers: to an older generation seeking to make sense of the changed environment for church-belonging today, and to a younger group wanting to explore their doubts over religious faith. *Free To Believe* is a continuation of that dialogue but with a different starting point and a different focus. Although it does not tackle traditional issues of theodicy, such as the problem of evil, it attempts to clarify what may block people from being psychologically free for faith. It then moves on to how the roads to faith can be rendered credible in our culture. Finally it tries to imagine how Christianity can be received and lived today. If *Help my Unbelief* was concerned with explicit problems of religious meaning and church-belonging, *Free To Believe* explores the more silent obstacles implicit in contemporary culture. It starts from another face of unbelief – not so much atheism as that spiritual lostness which is so characteristic of our time.

Behind this book lies my own pastoral experience with its mixture of gratitude, exasperation and hope. The gratitude is obvious enough: it was always a privilege to listen to young people expressing something of their deeper selves and of their limbo of uncertainty about faith. The exasperation comes from the fact that their vocabulary of faith was often so restricted – seldom through any fault of their own. They seemed to have received an overdose of conformist practices, moral codes and bits of undigested dogma, with the result that most talk about religion gravitated round these limited horizons. They seemed undernourished in any deeper language of searching. So the hope was born to explore another way of approaching the Christian vision for today, through taking a long journey towards its meaning. I decided to attempt a book that might avoid narrowly churchy confines and open a broader agenda for them. I wanted to evoke a richer sense of Church than they have encountered, through drawing on the tradition of faith reflected through the centuries.

In short, this book aims to serve various purposes:
(1) to broach a different apologetics or imaginative journey towards faith;
(2) to offer nourishment for believers who wish to support their always fragile faith;
(3) to be a practical manual on how to escape unfreedom in its many disguises.

But most of all, I would like this book to be worthy of my many 'less religious' friends. I want it to do justice to their struggles to make sense of life, their honesty in saying 'no thanks' to much of the religion they perceive. I would be happy if these pages assisted anyone in their struggle to escape into new freedom. Indeed I might adapt a famous saying of Cardinal Newman. If I were asked to offer a toast to truth. I might be tempted to reply: 'Let us drink to freedom first, and to truth afterwards'.

HOW TO READ THIS BOOK?

The short answer is – make it your own. Let it help you discover your story of escape-quest-love. By being in a certain sequence these chapters seek to provide you with a map towards a possible decision of faith. It is as if you were to phone for travel advice on a holiday weekend. You would be told what seems the best route to follow to avoid delays and difficulties. But this guidance will not get you to your destination; you have to do the travelling yourself.

My hope is that you will pause frequently while travelling these pages, not only to check the map but to relax and relish the scenery more personally. The ten 'scaffolding' sections at the end of each 'step' are explicitly designed to invite some such response – like picnic areas at the side of the road. They offer further ways of working at each of the stages. Sometimes they suggest exercises of meditation or imagination. Sometimes they draw upon the thoughts and writings of others, as a means of bringing in larger and more specialist horizons.

Friends who read drafts of this book, and to whom I am most grateful for their help, liked the snippets of quotations, peppered through my own argument. So I took the risk of including plenty of them, often without comment. They are meant to be traps for thought, like 'slow down' signs on the road. They are also an acknowledgement of my indebtedness to authors who have walked this way before. I have simply gathered my own synthesis from a wider and more ancient wisdom, in the hope of sharing it with fellow searchers of today.

A Self-Story as Prologue

My daily prayer is that I be true to my own inner world, that I do not become stunted.   Hermann Hesse

Dear Self,

If this book of yours is ever finished, it will in itself be a monument of faith. It will have been born against the odds, after labour long and hazardous.

Take tonight for instance. You sat at the end of the jetty, alone beside the sea in the evening sun, having escaped (that word again) there in 'foul humour'. Only this morning you had begun to draft this 'escape book' at long last. You had many pages from last summer when you first nibbled at this metaphor of freedom and unfreedom. But all day today nothing went right. Sentences became suffocated in their verbiage. In the late afternoon you arrived at the point of feeling that if there were many more days like this one, you might as well throw in the towel as a writer.

And the evening meal with the community didn't exactly alleviate the let-down. Everyone else seemed to be planning to go out to a film (because all the cinemas were offering a special £1 entry tonight). You wanted to go but then for two reasons you didn't. First, they didn't ask you: they assumed you would go if you wanted to, but they didn't actually invite you. Second, you doubted your own capacity to enjoy anything this evening, so dark the inner clouds. You let the moment slide and they all departed. Nothing remained except a visit to the jetty, perhaps a prayer down there in your favourite place, certainly a time to ponder the day, protected from phones and people.

So down you went – to sulk: let's be honest. You brought a book about faith, almost as a shield against the shadow

self. Phrases like 'mid-life strandedness' flowed through your
active brain on the way down. At least you could see your
'pain' in perspective, having just before the evening meal
browsed through an article about the famine in Africa and
about the failure of aid to make an impact on the tragedy
there. Once on the jetty, there was solitude of a peaceful sort
in the setting sun, until someone came sauntering down 'your'
jetty, and worse still, someone you knew. He was not looking
for you but just happened to stroll that way, and stopped and
talked. At first you found him unwelcome and suggested that
the far side of the pier was more sheltered from the wind. But
he stayed and talked and, as if prompted by fate, asked if you
were going to write another book – because he had greatly
liked the last one. The intruder suddenly became more
welcome. You mentioned, modestly, that you had tried to
begin another book this very morning, and were disappointed
with the first day's work. He went on to say how much he
admired people who manage to do so much, with writing
added in on top of many other commitments. Were you heard
purring or was it the low murmur of the motor-boat nearby?
At last he decided to continue his walk and to take your
advice about the less windy side. He went off, leaving you
alone and strangely changed.

You opened your book on faith and browsed through it. It
spoke about God often being thought of as outside experience,
outside the world, controlling everything from a distance. But
no: he was right here within people, his presence known
especially where there was some flash of resurrection in us,
some transformation of pain into peace. Ten minutes
previously you might have dismissed those words as wishy-
washy. Now they were reaching a more receptive reader.
They were finding an echo in the little drama that had just
happened to you. You had begun to hope again. You had
regained some faith in your own possibilities – a flicker at
least of resurrection.

You wanted then to go back to the typewriter. But first
you paused and prayed a moment, asking that what you were
attempting might be blessed, might be worthy of the struggles
of so many people who search to make sense, and often get
'stuck' – as you had been today.

And then on the way back something happened at the

railway bridge. Just four steps from the bottom stood three women, two youngish and the third elderly and frail. The old lady suddenly addressed you. It was not clear what she was saying but the gist was to ask you to stand there and catch her if she were to fall. She had already come down some fifteen steep steps, but had now suddenly lost her nerve and got stuck. For some reason she had more confidence in the stranger at the foot of the stairs than in her two (as I imagine) daughters. So you stopped and watched as she successfully descended the remaining steps. She waved a thank-you.

How easy to lose confidence. How easy to restore it – sometimes. As when this evening's word of support and moment of being needed gave you something of a flash of resurrection.

You will become stuck many times as you draft these pages. You will lose faith in what you set out to do. But you will also escape from prisons of unfaith again and again, so that the experience of writing this book will not be far from its central concerns: the continual battle for freedom; the constant quest for what is right; the discovery that everything can be rooted in love. When the darker moments come, remember that great poem by George Herbert called 'The Flower', where he expresses an emergence from despair into aliveness as a flower coming out of the death of winter into the blossom-time of spring:

> Who would have thought my shrivel'd heart
> Could have recover'd greennesse?
>
> . . . . .
>
> It cannot be
> That I am he
> On whom thy tempests fell all night.

The experience behind that poem is also an escape story – and a quest story and even a love story.

Part 1

Escape Stories

Earlier, in the course of the introduction, I outlined the typical plot of those escape stories from the Second World War, suggesting that they could serve as parables of a journey towards faith. To evoke the very scenario of imprisonment suggests that unfreedom can reign in my life and in our world – unless I resist it and struggle to escape. It implies that life itself is a multi-layered struggle to be free. Because there seems to be something wrong with humanity, freedom does not simply happen: I have to choose to make it happen. Otherwise I stay imprisoned in ways I may not even recognize. Above all, the escape story suggests that there will be several stages on any road to faith.

From my listening to people over the years and reflecting on their searchings, I think of four 'escape stories' that must happen before a person can confront questions about God's existence. Each person can be seen as inhabiting four worlds and each of these worlds can become a place of imprisonment and hence of blockage on any road to faith:

(1) a world of self – where one is either in touch with one's own depth or not;

(2) a social world – which can shape one's horizon and attitude in many ways;

(3) a world of inquiry – which can do justice to the question of God or else remain at a level of external argument;

(4) a world of religious images – where one's picture of God can be either true or distorted.

The chapters that follow will examine these four worlds and in particular the various ways in which freedom can be lost and, more importantly, regained.

Step 1

The First Freedom: From False to True Self

Through each day of each life flows the fascinating river that is called consciousness. Sometimes that stream is smooth, clear, calm; at other times it is churned up, muddy, rough. It is here that the Mood War is fought, that inner battle which has a hidden influence on everyone's freedom. In these pages we explore how people have recognized themselves as caught in some inner prison and yet found ways of emerging into the freedom of the true self; and without arriving at this freedom no real journey towards faith can start. It is said that Mrs Beeton began one of her celebrated recipes with the basic advice: 'first catch your hare'. Our topic in these pages is: first find your false self and then you will have some chance of discovering your true self.

THE DISCOVERY OF INIGO

He had two selves within him apparently, and they must learn to accommodate each other . . . some of us, with quick alternate vision, see beyond our infatuations. George Eliot

To illustrate the battle of dispositions we go back some four centuries to another soldier who found himself, almost without knowing it, involved in a different bid for freedom. This story took place in the north of Spain in the year 1521. What happened to one man then set a headline that has influenced thousands of people since; what he experienced and what he discovered through his experience became a classic adventure of how to arrive at inner freedom. The man's name was Inigo, and he was a mixture of courtier and

soldier; although nearly thirty years old he had remained a
bit of a drifter until this episode opened new horizons for him.

The beginning was nothing extraordinary for a soldier of
those times: his leg was broken by a cannon ball in battle
and he was carted home to recover if he could. Within a
month of the injury he was near death. Then he rallied and
managed to survive three grim operations (without anaes-
thetic). The battle had taken place on Whit Monday. All
through a hot summer he lay in torment. When the beautiful
Spanish autumn came, he was on the mend and decidedly
bored at having to stay so long in bed. But it was the only
way for the mutilated leg to set. Out of his restlessness and
boredom came a desire for distractions of some kind and this
in turn was to lead to his surprising discovery.

Lying now in his family house in the village of Loyola, he
wanted to while away the hours by feeding his fantasy life
with the popular love stories of those days, and he asked for
some of the silly tales of high romance that were in vogue at
the court. But the village of his home was not the court and
nothing of that kind could be found. His family could only
provide him with books about saints and about Christ. Out
of sheer boredom he took them up and played with the fan-
tasies they provoked in him. He gradually evolved a habit of
passing the time through two kinds of fantasy: he would give
space to imagining the life of the court and his romantic-cum-
sexual possibilities there, and then with equal intensity he
would enter into a daydream of becoming like the saints
(as in these religious books). Boredom was banished for the
moment, as these various images unfolded within him. Inigo
had discovered in himself a great capacity for interior cinema
and he ran the two films again and again, with many variations, through those late months of 1521.

But he was on the point of a greater discovery than how
to beat bedridden boredom. He recounts later how 'one day
it dawned on him' that there was 'a difference in his two
subjects for thought'. Both of them gave him equal absorption
and pleasure at the time, but when he set his imaginings
aside a crucial difference of response emerged. Only in the
aftermath of his fantasy periods, could he come to realize that
the courtly images left him feeling empty and dissatisfied in
himself, whereas with the religious images 'the joy remained

unabated even when he stopped thinking of them'. Let him speak for himself in words from his third-person autobiography that sound remarkably modern:

when he noticed the difference . . . he began to wonder at it. He understood from experience that one subject of thought left him dejection, while the other left him joy. This was his first ever insight into things of a spiritual kind. And later on, when he had gone through spiritual exercises, this experience was the starting point for teaching his followers how to discern between one spirit and another.

His seemingly simple discovery has a revealing pattern to it. If I am to become free of the false self, I have first to become aware of a flux within me; until that conflict of moods comes to consciousness little of inner freedom will be possible. Everyone experiences the daily ebb and flow of moods but many may never manage to pinpoint the conflict of those currents or to learn from that contrast of wavelengths within each self. But in fact, following the Inigo experience, it is quite easy to bring this hidden mood war into the light of awareness. The reader can try it even in a quick moment of self-reflection. Out of what level of myself is most of today being lived? Out of surface desires and immature rhythms of response? If so, the unmistakable sign will be some version of gnawing fatigue, some shadow of dissatisfaction and restlessness. Or is today being lived from a different rootedness and a different openness of vision? If so, the proof will be there as a sense of being-in-tune. There will be a deeper peace that can cope serenely with the everyday burdens of a crowded and seemingly scattered life.

What gives Inigo's words their modern ring is that he is recording his own experience and his stumbling into insight on the basis of that self-experience. It is his story of escape from the prison of a false and immature self through finding a neglected and truer self within him. In his own way he came to realize, as Erich Fromm was to put it, that destructiveness is the outcome of unlived life; he recognized his unlived life only when he learned to listen to a neglected layer of his own humanity. That contrast of wavelengths within him was his first key to freedom. Or in the language of Inigo (or Ignatius Loyola as he came to be known), each person

experiences an inner conflict between consolation and desolation and, more importantly, it is possible to learn to understand this conflict – a skill called discernment of spirits. Even
if that spiritual vocabulary seems remote from modern ways
of thinking, the underlying wisdom is far from irrelevant
today. It lies at the heart of any escape to freedom on the
level of consciousness. Indeed I have atheist friends who have
been greatly helped by this shatteringly simple insight of
Inigo. I can think of one marriage that was saved by it, or
another major life decision that could easily have been made
out of false consciousness if the person concerned had not
come to know the tradition of discernment initiated by Inigo.
His personal experience became a source of wisdom for others
because he pondered it prayerfully and only later came to see
its application for other people's struggles.

APPLYING HIS INSIGHT

*Most of us have to get in touch with ourselves first, to get into a
full relationship with ourselves before we can turn openly to our
relationship with God.*   John Main

The pattern of Inigo's discovery could be viewed as a ladder
with four rungs:
(1)   There exists an alternation of moods within each person
and it is not merely random or meaningless.
(2)   To become aware of this flux is an essential step towards
self-freedom.
(3)   By experiencing this contrast, which is called consolation and desolation, I can recognize a continual struggle
within me between a true and a false self;
(4)   This self-learning becomes practical and fruitful when I
obey the golden rule: good decisions can only come from the
true self; bad decisions spring from the pressures and panics
of the false self; therefore never make a decision when 'down'.
   The relevance of the Inigo discovery is wider than has been
touched on so far. It provides a master key for any struggle
of the inner self to escape from prisons of various kinds. This
is so even for a totally secular consciousness; but his wisdom
has a particular application to those in quest of religious

meaning. From the Inigo perspective it is the beginning that is all important. The first step on a journey towards faith is not what people often think it to be. It is not a matter of intellect alone; nor is it a matter of will alone. It may not even be a matter of prayer or of searching the Scriptures. Faith is a decision – to admit a strange truth about love. A good decision needs the freedom of the true self. Therefore faith cannot be arrived at when the false self is in the driving seat. It may require a prior struggle on the level of basic disposition, and this in turn needs recognition of the battle zones within each person.

But how am I to arrive at such a recognition? With the same tools that Inigo had – the imagination and the interplay of self-images. One set of images sought to keep him stuck in the habits of the past; the other images invited him into new awareness of who he was and what he could become. Any journey of escape from the ingrained patterns of the past depends on discovering this divided self, through the contrast of true and false consciousness.

For readers of these pages, whether believers or unbelievers in a religious sense, recounting the Inigo experience is intended as an invitation to try one's own journey of discovery through awareness. It is not an argument that will trap you into something which you do not want to accept. It does not ask you to go beyond what lies within your own self right now – even as you read. It could provide you with a map to a well-travelled road of self-wisdom. All it asks is that you give time to attending to your inner experience. Don't expect your efforts to pay dividends at once. It may take some time and some solitude (after all Inigo was months in bed) before any dawning recognition arrives. But if you stay at it, self-insight will come in some way. You will uncover a conflict of calls within you. You will become aware of the daily downward tug of a surface self, with its imprisoning habits of response. You will also become conscious of another possibility: to live from another source within you. And all this is verifiable in your experience over time. If you give it a fair trial (which means self-patience mainly), the Inigo plot will be re-enacted in you. By their fruits you will know the difference between the two 'spirits' as he called them. One set of images and responses will leave only vague unease or emptiness behind – and that is the signal of 'desolation' or the false self. Another set of images and responses will put you in touch with a freedom and a fullness that seems to last – and that is the sure sign of 'consolation' or the true self.

FROM ANGEL TO DEMON: PAINS OF SELF-KNOWING

Every one of us is shadowed by an illusory person: a false self . . . The way to find the real 'world' is not merely to measure and observe what is outside us, but to discover our own inner ground . . . in my deepest self. Thomas Merton

Without being unduly autobiographical these few pages hope to use my own personal experience as a way of making the Inigo insight more concrete. Far from being a success story, it is one of embarrassing unsteadiness. But it is a story of striving unevenly through the years to listen to the deeper realities and to live from that listening. Although the paralysis of routine often took over, something always rekindled the bigger desires. I have been rescued again and again from the habit of half-living.

On the eve of my taking what in the Jesuits we call 'final vows' (in 1978), I remember spending some of the day reading back through notebooks that I had kept over the previous fifteen years or so. They were spiritual journals of a personal kind, jottings of self-reflection covering many different situations. These notebooks, of many shapes and sizes, did not consist of regular entries. Sometimes months would have passed without anything being set down; nevertheless they did form a fascinating record of struggles and discoveries over the years. I had never taken the time to peruse them all in one sitting, but on that day it seemed appropriate to look back and to gather the fruits. What I found was like a refrain running through the years. It was as if in vastly different contexts I was still the same self, with the battle-lines of imprisonment and freedom having a strange similarity all the time. Some of the entries were written during periods of intense study, other in times of much activity. Some of them came from times of dullness, others from days of excitement. Some dealt with happenings within myself and known only to me; others involved relationships, friendships, events of pain or happiness shared with other people. But through all the variety was one recurring theme, like a motif in music, and one that surprised me on that day of rereading in 1978. It was my slower re-living of the Inigo experience.

Just as he discovered a surface level of himself that was in danger of smothering his unknown hunger, I too experienced a pendulum within me between two quite different moods of life. My most frequent word for one of these was 'the performer' and the favourite term for the other side was 'the child'. By 'performing' I meant a compulsion to appear successful and to impress people. It was a long story, going back no doubt to my proud parents and their healthy enough desire to see me 'do well'. The little boy who would be put on display at home to play the piano for visitors (and interestingly I never play it now) later developed many ways of feeding his need for praise. What started out innocently enough became a habit, even an addiction. Right through my secondary school period I learned to play that success game in a highly competitive spirit: success in studies or drama or debating served as a shield to hide the other self that felt unlikeable, inadequate, and particularly useless at the other kind of games. But I was partly saved from this 'prig' side of me through friendships, some at school and more importantly in my four years of university. The 'performer' did not disappear, but the 'child' escaped from prison and learned to trust his feelings, to allow playfulness, to reach intimacy, and to enjoy a non-performing belonging with others.

I was well into my thirties on that day in 1978 when I clarified something of the battlelines of my life. They had their roots back in childhood, and the battle is still waging in mid-life. My little cluster of compulsions and freedoms could be expressed in many ways. Sometimes those notebooks spoke of 'control' as the negative factor, as the demon behind the 'performer'; at other times they spoke of 'idolatry' – the false self wanting to be the centre of attention. Down through the years I evolved a varied vocabulary for expressing this shadow side of myself. The list of self-accusations is long: I was a fraud, intolerant, unreliable in my commitments, mean and arrogant. The positive sides seemed to call forth less eloquence of expression: belonging, non-striving, trusting, enjoying, able to listen to God and to liberate others. These were my ways of putting words on my experience of flux. That flux continues and no doubt it will always have some of the same characteristics. That is what shapes me. I range from angel to demon and, thank God, back again. On one side is a tense and worried self, part Narcissus and part Hitler, capable of both sulks and savagery. On the other side is someone with a reverence before God and humanity, able to enter into the flow of life and even to enjoy skirmishes with now familiar demons. This truer self is equally real, if often submerged under the tiredness of the struggle and the pressures of the situation around. But knowing the battlelines is the beginning of freedom; in this sense my different lifestory is an echo and verification of the Inigo discovery. Indeed it was through him that I learned how to listen to personal reality in this way.

The hope of these pages is that my own experience, and his, may trigger off a similar self-discovery for the reader. The life-context may not be the same and the personality may be quite different. But something of this mood war exists within everyone, and the first freedom is to recognize it. Moods may seem like interior weather, largely uncontrollable, and yet they are more like flowers and weeds in a garden: with a little bit of attention, the weeds can be kept in their place and then the flowers can flourish. In the mood war, with its constant flux of 'consolation' and 'desolation', awareness is the first and crucial weapon, allowing me to catch a glimpse of the two selves, and so to know my particular angels and demons. Any moment of struggle, however minor, can be an occasion for making this discovery of the two selves within. That is the Inigo road to freedom. He came to believe that desolation may be inevitable and even fruitful as a passing phenomenon, but it is not meant to be long-lasting. A desolation that lingers can be destructive. Inigo would insist that consolation is our natural state, not necessarily in the sense of intense feelings of aliveness, but at least in the sense that the flow of life can be outgoing towards goodness, creativity, love. All this is intended to put flesh on the old spiritual wisdom that inner struggle is due to a divided self. But if this is true, another question remains: how can you go further than simply recognizing two wavelengths within? How can you struggle to escape, in practice, from the false to the true self?

AWAKENING TO THE POSSIBLE

Attention animated by desire is the whole foundation of religious practices. Simone Weil

My attention is often or even most of the time captured by outside forces. E. F. Schumacher

Before any such journey can be undertaken, a person has to see the need for it. Just as there were some war-prisoners who had settled comfortably enough into prison life, so there can be many people who never awaken to what their lives lack. The starting-point here is some healthy dissatisfaction with one's own status quo. This is the stage described by Kierkegaard as the transition from an 'aesthetic' or drifting existence where everything is chosen (or rather not chosen) on a basis of searching for pleasure and avoiding pain. Sooner or later that existence fails to satisfy. Sooner or later something happens to cause that edifice to crumble, as with Inigo in bed after his cannon-ball, when the outer casualty forced him to a situation where he was less able to avoid wondering, and where he came to realize the shallowness of what he had previously had as the centre of his hopes. He moved out of the 'aesthetic' or immature level of existing through hearing a deeper call of his own true self.

What can arouse the smothered hunger of a self that is adrift? Something has to happen to shake the complacency of the self-system. Few people will have their legs broken in battle. Few will have the luxury of months of solitude. And yet there can be many equivalents of Inigo's cannon-ball and Inigo's bed. A period of routine living or half-living is interrupted by some unexpected joy or pain. That is the key to new wondering. That experience offers the possibility for new self-insight.

I can vouch for the truth of this in my own life, and not always in powerful or dramatic ways. I recall one weekend when a coincidence of encounters awoke me to new awareness. It involved three rather different kinds of experience. The first significant challenge to my routine consciousness was a meeting with a young married couple who were in a state of huge happiness; they had just completed a series of workshops on spiritual companionship and the whole event left them bubbling with hope and with generosity, and able to gather me into the contagion of their joy. It was not a transitory 'high': it was a glimpse of what is possible when the true self is fully alive. The second experience was liberating in a different way. A close friend arrived, whom I had not seen for some years, and after some initial awkwardness we both admitted that we had got hurt by a distance between us and that we were both a little afraid of this reunion. This mutual truth set us free for what became an occasion of reconciliation between us and renewal of life within each of us. The third blessing of that weekend came at first with pain, with the news that a young man whom I had known well as a student was in hospital and dying. I hurried in to visit him and was shocked by finding him almost too weak to speak. After a few minutes he managed to say in a strong voice, 'I know I could die but I want to live'. That was the beginning of one of the most quietly powerful conversations of my life, and in fact my last real conversation with him before his death. I left that hospital awoken again. I had come to give comfort and in fact received much more than I could give. And the same was true of the other moments too. To run into depth in others is to be humbled and set free for the depths in one's own self. They were cannon-balls for me over one unusual weekend.

Paradoxically it is possible to be struck by cannon-balls and avoid going to bed. It is possible to experience these invitations to depth in a merely passing and 'aesthetic' manner. If some version of cannon-ball is the potential awakener of consciousness imprisoned in dullness, it requires some version of lying-in-bed before the false self can emerge into new freedom. And that is the focus of the remainder of this chapter – how to get to bed!

SCAFFOLDING FOR AWARENESS

I have trouble being still, and furthermore my hope is based upon getting to be still so that the axial lines can be found. When striving stops, the truth comes as a gift.   Saul Bellow

As mentioned in the introduction, each 'step' will end with some 'scaffolding'. Because the first step is so crucial what is offered here will be more extensive than anywhere later in the book. If I fail to find a key to the centre of the self, all subsequent struggling to escape could prove unreal. But if I can make the transition from half-listening to really listening, the way is open for further freedoms and searchings.

These pages will try to show that practical skills exist to help one to win the war of the inner self. It will be a magpie section in that most of its suggestions are gathered from here and there in the long tradition of interiority. I have often found that the experience of prayer is a topic of unusual interest to my more unbelieving friends; where beliefs, belongings and practices may divide us, this area of inner life can be a bridge between us. The reason is not hard to find. Everyone suffers from scatteredness, and yet everyone wants more stillness. Therefore any wisdom is welcome that might offer help towards a more gathered self.

In fact most problems over prayer have little to do with faith itself: they have to do with the pray-er, the state of the person who tries to reach out to God. Most of the time I find myself, for various reasons, unready or unripe. 'The readiness is all,' said Hamlet, to be closely echoed by 'ripeness is all' in *King Lear*. The best initial advice concerning prayer deals with skills of self-readying.

I have found that some strategies of the East offer immense help towards inner stillness. More than once I have surprised some student, who had come to consult me about not being able to concentrate on work, by asking him or her to lie down on a mat on the floor of my office, so that I could see them taking a deep breath! As expected I found that most of them were 'chest breathing' rather than 'diaphragm breathing'; so I would place a large volume of Shakespeare on their abdomen and tell them to move it up and down as they breathed in and out. After the predictable panic of wondering whether I was sane, they would gradually relax and find a quietly powerful rhythm of deep breathing that banished a lot of their tensions. The trouble was that they were starting their quest for 'concentration' in the wrong quarter – in some gymnastics of will-power. But the wisdom of the East would say: 'Lose your mind and come to your senses.' Certainly most skills of stillness that I have found helpful start with some focus on the physical senses, as in the experience of breathing.

A more subtle variation on that experience is what I call the 'prayer of the breath', adapted from the Buddhist tradition. This involves paying attention to the coming and going of the air through one's nose. At first it seems wiser to focus on the sensation of the incoming cool breath as it touches the warmer skin of the inner nostrils. If one counts five breaths and repeats this a few times, one will become increasingly aware of the gentle movement of the air as it enters. Then one can turn one's attention to the outgoing breath which is a more delicate vibration of the warmer air returning. As in all these efforts, self-patience is essential: it takes time to focus and to relax into awareness of this kind, and anything less than about ten minutes is likely to be futile. Gradually you find that you can be gathered by this one focus of awareness, and that it can banish other distractions. Once a certain steady focus on the sensation of the coming and going of the breath has been established, it is possible to build on that awareness, letting it become a kind of prayer. Each breath in can be experienced as a gift and can evoke a sense of gratitude. Similarly each breath out can be felt as a response, a giving back. It is important not to lose the root-edness in sensation and above all not to escape into thoughts. Let the rhythm of the breathing and the sensation of the nostrils remain the anchor; this primary awareness can expand into an attitude of thanksgiving and belonging, where the breath itself can seem to be praying within you.

ANCHORING IN THE PRESENT

What is called 'onepointedness' is nearly always the basis of Eastern methods of meditation. Their secret is no secret really: it simply says that if you give time to a definite focus of awareness, it can act as a sure guide into a state of stillness and one strangely easy to arrive at. In cold print these descriptions can seem artificial and unreal, but if practised they are surprisingly helpful in creating that outer and inner quiet so often rendered problematic by the rhythms of our culture. The particular fruit of all these skills of stillness is that they help to root us in the present moment. Since anxieties and distractions generally come from the past or the future, it is a great benefit to find a method of anchoring awareness in the now.

The body's senses provide one of four focus points of this kind. The three other areas that can serve to gather one's awareness are: (i) the world of words; (ii) the flow of feelings or emotions; and (iii) the power of imagination or the inner cinema that we spoke of with Inigo. If not channelled towards self-unity, any of these four can offer fertile ground for distractions. Imagine yourself settling down to have some period of hoped-for inner quiet. If you make no decision to 'centre' yourself in some way, one or other of these four families of awareness will surely cause distraction. You will become preoccupied about the sounds around or the stiffness in your neck (sensation). You will find yourself full of chatter, shaping imaginary conversations (words). You might find yourself strongly aware of some anger which has been lurking behind the busyness of the day (emotions). Or you could discover that you are picturing yourself miles away in some other situation (images). In this way each of these sources of awareness can become an enemy, depriving you of any anchor for steady stillness. But these potential enemies can, if properly cultivated, become allies and friends. They can become the key to escaping from the prison of mere scatteredness.

Words can scatter or they can gather: use of a 'mantra' has become a well-known method in recent times in the West. This means taking a word or a set of words and repeating them in silence as a road into awareness of one's core self. Nor is this approach unique to the East. As far back as the fourteenth century the anonymous author of *The Cloud of Unknowing* suggested taking a small but profound word like 'love' or 'God' and saying it over and over within oneself.

Similarly emotions, especially negative ones such as anger,

can kidnap the inner self, with the result that any attempt at quiet awareness only opens a door into turmoil. If so, the only escape route is through self-truth, and this means staying with the painful feelings and passing through them into some kind of slow honesty and costly peace.

Everyone has some capacity for fantasy, even if they have not the same power of imagination as Inigo. There are also many ways of harnessing this gift in order to escape from a surface self and into deeper awareness. I recall one young man on a directed retreat, who was trying to pray in the traditional manner of words-and-thoughts and who was beset by 'distractions' of a powerfully visual kind. He would imagine himself swimming through dark caves, running up against sharp rocks, yet invited forward by a golden light and the ocean beyond. All this seemed to him to be irrelevant nonsense, an obstacle to his prayer. But what if it could be accepted as a way of praying? What if these images were not distractions but significant symbols of the hurts and hopes of his life? Some psychological schools encourage people to identify themselves in imagination with, for instance, a rose-bush: where is it growing? What roots does it have? How does it change through the seasons? Such basic images, often drawn from the four elements, serve at least two purposes. They concentrate the self, leading to focus and stillness. They also awaken self-images, bringing basic conflicts into the light of awareness.

All these approaches, and many others, can be tools for tunnelling out of the prison of the false self. They can serve in the struggle of each person to find the 'still point' of his or her life. They can unite believers and unbelievers at this first step of escaping from unfreedom of the self. Both those who believe in God and those who cannot do so are equally in need of glimpsing

> The calm existence that is mine when I
> Am worthy of myself
> 　　　　　　(William Wordsworth)

Thus they are united in trying to defeat the unworthiness of the false self, and to enter ways of calm awareness so that the true self can be set free. And that is the only sure starting point for a journey towards faith.

This whole first step can be summed up in a anecdote about the conductor Herbert von Karajan. Asked once about how he managed to lift an orchestra into such unity and inspiration, he recalled a moment in his childhood when he was learning horse-jumping. The night before his first attempt he lay awake terrified, wondering how he would be able to get this huge animal up and over the fence. Then it came to him that all he had to do was set it in the right position and it would lift itself.

Step 2

Seeing through the System

We who are born into the world's artificial system can never adequately know how little in our present state and circumstances is natural . . . It is only through the medium of the imagination that we lessen those iron fetters which we call truth and reality, and make ourselves even partially sensible of what prisoners we are.

Nathaniel Hawthorne

JOINING THE RESISTANCE

Our first escape occurs within the self. It is like that moment in the wartime stories when someone wakes up to the fact that they do not have to stay in prison. It involves a change of inner attitude from dullness to aliveness, from avoiding feelings to being in touch with them. Our second escape is different. It has less to do with the self than with society. In terms of those prison stories, it is more akin to the long period of preparing to escape; they had to study the system in order to beat it. So too with us today who may be kidnapped within social systems that spurn and even stifle our religious potentials.

I remember talking to a Polish priest at the time of the resurgence of national feeling through Solidarity. I asked him how it was that religion seemed so universally popular in Poland whereas in the 'free world' it is largely in decline as an influence in society. His answer was unhesitating and crystal clear: 'We in Poland have a visible enemy to human values in a totalitarian state, but you in the West have an enemy that you cannot identify so clearly – all the allurements of a superficial lifestyle'. The implication was that if only we could see our enemy, and know his power, we too would form a new Solidarity. We would want to join the Resistance.

If prison by definition is a context that tries to prevent escape, it is possible to view much of the cultural environment of today an an imprisoning force. Go back to our typical escapes from war-time prisons. In spite of huge variety of situations, all those adventures had one predictable feature: preparedness through watching the enemy. One had to know the movements of the guards and indeed one had to find out as much as possible about their attitudes, duty rosters, and likely counter-escape plans. If 'know the enemy' was the motto for any successful escapee, it is also the challenge of two of the parables of Jesus (both of them in Luke 14). One tells of a man who wants to build a tower: suppose he forgets to do any planning about it and about how many bricks he may need, then he might never get beyond the foundations and people will laugh at his unfinished tower. Side by side with that is the story of the king going to war against another king: he will have to make sure that he is not greatly outnumbered by his opponent who is marching against him. If that is the case, he might be wiser to negotiate for peace and avoid an inevitable defeat.

What these parables and escape stories have in common is preparedness, inner and outer: fail to prepare, prepare to fail. It is one thing to achieve some inner freedom and to get in touch with the true self; it is another thing to survive a hostile world, where spiritual freedom has no 'cash value' and may even prove too innocent in its personalism. To move towards mature faith today, I may need to suspect some forces of falsity installed in the driving seat of society around me. More than that, I may need to cultivate a healthy hostility towards the prevailing culture – something strong among imaginative writers of this century.

THREE CAUTIONARY TALES

The world around us has its roots in an established disorder, which makes the mere proclamation of the gospel subversive.

Oscar Romero

Are we as free in modern society as we like to think? Between 1921 and 1948 three quite similar novels appeared, one in each decade, and all three answered this question in the negative. Each writer took an anti-utopian stance, in that he explored a so-called ideal future and found it not only wanting but dangerous. Two of these books are well known – Aldous Huxley's *Brave New World* (1932) and George Orwell's *Nineteen Eighty-Four* (1949). But the earliest and in many ways the most impressive of the trio was *We* (1921) by Yevgeny Zamyatin. This novel seems to have been a significant influence on the two later authors: Huxley probably knew it and Orwell openly acknowledged his indebtedness. Zamyatin himself was a Russian author who fell foul of the authorities during the post-revolution regime, whose book was banned there, and who eventually died in poverty in Paris in 1937. Even his title implies that a collectivity of 'we' has ousted the individual 'I', and his story is narrated by D-503, the talented designer of a space-ship. He has begun to experience strange dreams which alienate him from the 'mathematically infallible happiness' of the One State. The plot tells how D-503 gradually becomes a subversive through both his relationship with I-330 (female) and his unresolved wondering about human reality. When he admits this condition to a doctor, the reply is 'You're in a bad way! Apparently you have developed a soul.' The only remedy is to submit to the Great Operation, now available for all numbers:

> The latest discovery of State Science is the location of the centre of imagination – a miserable little nodule in the brain in the area of the pons Varolii. Triple-X-ray cautery of this nodule – and you are cured of imagination – FOREVER.

At the close of the book this 'fantasectomy' delivers D-503 from all his inner turmoil and makes him able to denounce I-330 as one of the 'enemies of happiness'.

> Can it really be true that I once felt – or imagined that I felt – all this? . . . No delirium, no absurd metaphors, no feelings: nothing but facts. Because I am well, I am entirely, absolutely well. I smile – I cannot help smiling: a kind of

splinter was pulled out of my head . . . Because Reason must prevail.

In Zamyatin two faces of imprisonment come together, an oppressive surveillance and an imposed version of happiness. Orwell in his turn will expand on the first and Huxley on the second. When *Nineteen Eighty-Four* first appeared Aldous Huxley wrote to congratulate Orwell and to voice his more psychological view of the unfreedoms of the future:

> Whether in actual fact the policy of the boot-on-the-face can go on indefinitely seems doubtful. My own belief is that the ruling oligarchy will find less arduous and wasteful ways of governing and of satisfying its lust for power, and that . . . can be just as completely satisfied by suggesting people into loving their servitude as by flogging and kicking them into obedience.

Orwell himself was well aware of the differences between their visions. Some five years before writing *Nineteen Eighty-Four* he described *Brave New World* as 'a completely materialistic vulgar civilization based on hedonism', adding that he was more drawn to depict a 'slave state' of fear, one fuelled by 'literally continuous war'.

The two English novels have proved prophetic, as they dramatize in different ways how easily people can be controlled within systems of mindless uniformity. Orwell's more political tragedy continues to come true in the many totalitarian regimes of today. Huxley's satire exposes the opiates of the capitalist West, where an economy of consumption exercises its own benign but ruthless dictatorship. In *Brave New World* people are drugged into false happiness by doses of 'soma', the serenity-producing tablets (also available in spray form for emergencies). Surrounded by synthetic music, people are constantly provided with opportunities for sport, sex, and the 'feelies' – a techological entertainment of 'agreeable sensations'. In this tranquillized paradise 'solitude' becomes impossible and 'struggle' old-fashioned; where the College of Emotional Engineering can cater for all needs, 'religious sentiment is superfluous'. Rather like Zamyatin's D-503, the two rebel figures in *Brave New World* experience a deeper imagination at work in them and hence an 'unreplenished emptiness' even in the midst of the supposed rapture of a soma group. Ultimately Bernard rejects a life where 'nothing costs' anything: 'I don't want comfort. I want God, I want poetry, I want real danger, I want freedom, I want goodness. I want sin.... I'm claiming the right to be unhappy.'

Putting these three works side by side offers a fascinating contrast in pessimism. It also echoes the remark of my Polish friend who was wondering which would prove the more undermining enemy: the openly unfriendly regime or the culture of superficiality that rules the 'free world'. It is surely Huxley's vision of unfreedom that is the major obstacle to faith in the Western world today: we can be imprisoned in pleasant chains, that grip us without undue chafing and that hold us in half-life.

THE JUSTICE NOTE — A PERSONAL HISTORY

It happens that every man in a bank hates what the bank does, and yet the bank does it. The bank is something more than men, I tell you. It's the monster. Men made it, but they can't control it.

John Steinbeck

The religion I grew up with was very much a two-tiered affair, of belonging obediently to the church of my childhood and of this developing in the teenage years into a more personal relationship with Christ. As a university student I ran into many doubts, but what I had received earlier never totally collapsed. At the age of twenty-one I spent a challenging year in France, in a world where my kind of Catholicism was rare and even eccentric. I remain grateful for the broadening impact of that year, out of which a major choice became possible – the choice of a Jesuit vocation. So far, then, there were three notes in the chord of faith for me: belonging, believing, calling. I lived from these three notes for at least the first ten years of my Jesuit life and they are still the foundations of my faith-story. I remain happily faithful to the Church, with its warts and its wisdom. I have lived, however unsteadily, a life of personal prayer that nourishes my sense of God. And I have greatly enjoyed the adventure of trying to make the gospel vision credible and livable for a different generation.

The major change of the last ten years has been the gradual entry of a fourth note into the chord of my faith. This fourth note is less about Church, less about me, less about the gospel as true; rather it sees the gospel as a new way of living in society today. It could be called the 'justice note' within the chord of faith. For me it is only since ordination that this expanded interpretation of Christian faith began to have any impact. Now that I look back on my earlier and still deeply-rooted language of faith, it seems dangerously 'private' – a matter of God-and-me to a large extent. It is not a question of rejecting those deep roots but of escaping what may be narrow there. Faith today needs to wake up to the systems that surround us and to develop skills to see through their pressures. Otherwise it could be naive about the source of much of today's spiritual impotence.

In 1971 a Synod of Bishops in Rome studied the question of justice today and concluded that in our modern world the desire for justice would be frustrated if it ignored the 'systems of domination' and the 'objective obstacles which social structures place in the way of conversion of hearts'. I could give a vague assent to all this but the stress on systems and structures was alien to me. My spirituality at that time was too personalist to feel at home with this reading of reality.

Then in 1974 the Jesuit order had an important international meeting (called a General Congregation), when a new focus was chosen for our overall mission today. Asking themselves what was the call of God in this particular moment of history, that world-wide gathering arrived at a powerfully simple answer: the greatest need today was 'the service of faith' joined with 'the promotion of justice'. These two central struggles – to make faith real and to liberate from oppression – were in fact one struggle. Injustice was seen as a practical denial of God, and in so far as atheism deprives people of the possibilities of religious vision, it too can cause cultural injustice.

All this was an exciting theory. The trouble began when people asked how it was to be put into practice. By temperament and background I was more a 'faith man' than a 'justice man', in the sense that I felt at home in helping people to discover Christ in personal and spiritual ways. Through my university contacts I had plenty of exposure to individuals struggling to make sense of their lives or struggling over a religion which seemed to be fading for them. I had much less exposure to people in situations of poverty or deprivation, but then in 1976 I spent six months in India, much of it working in leper colonies and in Mother Teresa's home for the dying in Calcutta. During those months I soaked in the slow shock that poverty was not a minority phenomenon but a way of life for huge majorities. This is what they were talking about as a system or a structure. But I do not think that the penny dropped until I came home. I can still remember my revulsion when I saw the opulence of London shops and the thronged pubs of Dublin. 'Waste' became my word of most anger.

And yet that anger could remain unfruitful. The Indian experience and the contrast with the West had put me in a position to understand something of the established systems of injustice. I had taken a step from compassion for individuals (essential in itself) to a wider awareness of the social evil in the world today. But what to do about it? One answer was to hope to live more simply myself and to get others to do the same – with the aim of supporting development aid. I was no longer at ease with hand-outs. 'Give people fish today and they will be hungry tomorrow. Give them fishing nets and they may not be hungry tomorrow'. I remember arguing this on a television programme during Lent of 1977. All this was fine but some bridge remained to be built between what had been my language of faith and this new vision. Otherwise the 'fourth note' might never integrate itself into my spirituality.

I have written these last few pages because I believe that many people are now struggling with a similar transition from one model of faith to another. I also believe that if the language of faith is to be genuinely credible in our modern world, it has to do justice to the justice question; above all, it has to recognize the false systems that imprison us and can thwart the journey towards faith.

THE ANTHILL REVISITED

*We live in a secular world. To adapt to this world, the child
abdicates its ecstasy.* R. D. Laing

*To the business of business, God is irrelevant. He is not needed for
the success of the economic enterprise.* John Courtney Murray

In 1863 Dostoevsky spent some months visiting Europe and
on returning to Russia set down his *Winter Notes on Summer
Impressions.* His response was one of horror at the 'anthills'
which constituted the cities of the West. The poverty in
London's Whitechapel district shocked him, but he reserved
his strongest attack for the Crystal Palace, describing it as
another Babylon. This 'palace', built to house the Great Exhi-
bition, summed up for him all the ugliness and pride of an
industrial empire: 'A rich and ancient tradition of denial and
protest is needed in order not to yield . . . not to bow down
in worship of fact . . . not to take the actual for the ideal.'
Dostoevsky went further than voicing his dissent from the
prevailing system; he discerned the heart of the evil system
in 'the typically Western principle of individual isolation'.
This together with a 'desperate yearning, born of despair, to
retain the status quo' created a Europe ruled by 'self-seeking'.
Returning to Russia, Dostoevsky found himself pondering the
radical opposition between the way of life he had seen in the
West and the values of the gospel. This was the theme of his
'winter notes'.

In the summer of 1983 I spent two months in cities of the
United States. Although I had spent a happy year studying
in America in the late sixties, I had not returned since then;
perhaps my own perspectives had changed in that time –
with the entry of the 'justice note' I spoke of. All I know is
that from the outset of the 1983 visit, my response was more
negative – not to the people, whom I found exceptionally
welcoming, but to the system that I sensed enthroned. The
same system is enthroned in little Ireland but it was easier
to sniff it out in Manhattan. Without daring to emulate
Dostoevsky, I want to gather some other 'winter notes on
summer impressions' about the dominant culture in our
Western world. So these pages are not meant to be anti-

American. They are 'anti' all the sources of dehumanization that can rob us of our freedom.

About 150 years ago a Frenchman visited America and out of his nine-month stay came a celebrated book, of both admiration and critique, and one whose insights ring true even today. Alexis de Tocqueville arrived at the conclusion that in spite of appearances no other country had 'so little independence of mind and real freedom of discussion'. His *Democracy in America* also commented on the 'curiosity' of Americans as both 'insatiable and cheaply satisfied', and he added that their 'habit of inattention must be considered as the greatest defect'. What he discerned as a civilization of scatteredness (or what his compatriot Pascal had called *divertissement*) has since grown into a total economic system and way of life, primarily in North America but in fact throughout the world. In Herbert Muller's words we have 'the highest standard of low living in all history'. But these generalizations need focus, and our topic here is freedom for faith. Our concern is that a social system can induce a state of mind that becomes a blockage to religious belief of any genuine kind. And so to my impressions of 1983.

SOCIETY OF SUBTLE PROPAGANDA

> *Modern man is drinking and drugging himself out of awareness, or he spends his time shopping, which is the same thing.*
>
> Ernest Becker

> *I don't believe that most people are attracted to permanent illusion.*
>
> Christopher Koch

I would single out three main causes of unease and even alarm: the level of concealed propaganda as a source of social conformity; the machinery of constant self-satisfaction; and the manipulation of gospel truth through media religion. What I mean by propaganda can be illustrated by television in general and advertising in particular. Through the universality of television in the affluent world, a dominant ideology of spending and success is everywhere reinforced. Human reality is reduced to a perpetual fantasy. The huge scale of television culture means that showbiz sincerity becomes the language of truth. The pleasure-oriented images of that entertainment world cannot but induce a Huxley-like passivity in their audience. Most sinister of all, both producers and receivers can remain unaware of the dehumanizing effects of their entire system. The Big Lie is the freedom of the individual, which may be true in some external sense, but the pressures of commercial stimulation seem designed to rob people of any inner freedom and of any capacity for critique of the saturating values that come at them from every angle.

One of the shocks for the European in America is the omnipresence of advertising. I remember my amazement at finding almost every item of news on television followed by a commercial, or the weather-forecaster breaking his summary to tell us what gasoline to use in this heat. It is sometimes said that advertising has little impact on people, that it is like a background noise which one becomes accustomed to. But is big business so stupid as to spend billions on something that has no effect? Besides, my real objection is not to this continuous propaganda for artificial needs, but to the life-image that emerges. One advertisement that provoked me was for a 'new and meaty dietfood for overweight dogs'. To my mind, only a conscience cut off from the human realities of our world could contemplate promoting such a product. But conscience is not part of the fantasy person created by such commercials. Their ethic is the reverse of the Beatitudes. Happy are the glossy people – their bodies will be admired. Happy those with spare cash – for the moment they will be satisfied. Happy those who live with the latest novelty – they will have fun. Happy are the tough ones – they know how to get their way. And so on. Everywhere in our Western world commercials seek to make cowards of us all, by playing on our insecurities. When brought out into the open such values are both childish and idolatrous. Our question here is: If I am sucked into this system uncritically and let it imprison my imagination, what freedom will I have left to search for anything of the spirit?

Perhaps the dream world of advertising is an easy target, but it is an eloquent symbol of a culture devoted to superficial self-satisfactions. Another memory captures this for me – a picture on a plastic container for oversize pants, where a fat

man is saying, 'I'm on a seafood diet: everything I see I eat'.
Once again the overweight issue turns up, as if signifying an
affluent West fed to excess with wrong food. Something that
might seem amusing at first glance turns out to be sickening
on reflection. More importantly there is the implicit ideology
of hedonism: the good life is simply plenty of pleasure, even
irresponsible pleasure that damages one's health – but what
the hell!

In this light it becomes fascinating to turn to the selling of
the gospel through popular preachers and the media. Unlike
television or advertising, this is a peculiarly American
phenomenon so far; but it threatens to spread fast in coming
years. My horror story here is of an exorcism-by-radio show
that I happened to hear one Sunday morning. An alcoholic
phoned in willing to accept responsibility for his own
condition, only to be told in ringing tones that the alcoholic
demon was the only cause of his troubles and this demon
would now be cast out over the airwaves. As a hysterical
mumbo-jumbo began, I turned off in every sense, and felt
totally atheistic before that kind of god, who exists only in
human gullibility. As to the smoother performances of the
television evangelists, my reaction was more of agnosticism.
They sometimes say the right words. They are close to the
gospel at times. But their appeal is so much to pleasant
consolation (one show comes from a 'glass cathedral') and to
an unquestioning blessing of the status quo in society, that it
is hard to hear the voice of Christ there. Besides, money-
making seems so much a part of their operation that the Jesus
of the gospels would surely throw out these new invaders of
the temple.

If the system can dilute Jesus with such sugar and hijack
the values of the gospel to suit Mammon's many faces, then
we may suspect a new Babel, a human construction that is
ultimately anti-human. In terms of the argument of this book,
our faith potentials are sapped at their roots by a hidden form
of idolatry and, if so, we need to move from innocence to a
healthy suspicion of the systems around. As some Marxists
like to say, context conditions consciousness; so our journey
towards faith could prove futile unless we wake up to these
pressurizing contexts. Even to begin to look at the cultural
environment in this perspective casts new light on faith itself.

Christian faith is not just a question of truth but a way of
life, and a way of life that resists the norms of mass society.
The greatest victory for the consumer ideology is to reduce
religion to one more item on the supermarket shelf, making
Christianity compete in the supply and demand of comforts
and assurances. Thus a little bit of religion can become a
most successful *musak* or background feeling for a life of fundamental drift or immaturity. This tranquillizing use of religion
for human security is the most typical trap of the first world.
Christianity is turned into a pleasant evasion of reality,
personally consoling but unchallenging socially, attractive for
quick uplift and even a certain generosity, but avoiding the
depths of discipleship as a choice within today's world.

As Einstein said decades ago, we are surer about means
than about ends. Much of the time we are all unconscious
victims of our success as a technological culture. We are all
prisoners of unawareness, blind to the false values that we
may be blithely living. Take for instance the two contexts
within which my life has been lived – university work and
church ministry. I have been part of universities for a quarter
of a century now, either as student or teacher, and they are
places of enormous ambiguity today. They are elite establish-
ments that create their own forms of oppression, while
remaining blind, at least in practice (theory is something
else!), to the dangers of their own system. My fear is that in
the very area of the humanities where I have worked, I have
more often played a game of cleverness than paid the price
of genuine wisdom. I have doubts about the whole apparatus
of literary criticism (in which I became quite expert): does it
not train students in superficiality about depth? The
professional system rules but larger values are sacrificed.

In the church milieu other institutional temptations can
win the day: authority can be misused, people can be
unheard, and ritualism can pretend to be spiritual nourishment. The list could continue and it would be a rewriting of
the pages of the gospels where Christ confronts established
religion: the Pharisees did not die with that generation. Their
spirit shows itself whenever I fail as disciple and act instead
as manager of the things of God. Where the human seeks to
manage the divine strange results emerge – as will be seen in

our next section, which is on one of the perennial dangers of
religion, creating strange gods.

Seeing through the system is only a version of recognizing
humanity as fallen. Interestingly the story of the Fall in
Genesis is not just that of Adam and Eve – a story of a broken
relation with God. It is also the story of Cain and Abel –
about the breaking of bonds between brothers. And it is the
story of the building of Babel – the system of pride that
kidnaps human energies and causes us to miss our way. It is
that third face of evil that we have tried to explore here – as
a prison to be recognized, resisted, and if possible escaped
from.

SCAFFOLDING FOR REFLECTION

What is offered here is borrowed from three distinguished
authors in the area of cultural analysis. Two of them are
American Jesuits and the third is a French Calvinist
theologian.

William Lynch in *The Image Industries*, first published in
1959, gave a prophetic warning about the power of mass
media to impoverish human imagination through its
'flattened emotional range'. He saw a certain idolatry lurking
behind the glamour of the advertisements:

> What is being sold is not the thing but a hidden glory,
> the new *deus absconditus*, the hidden God . . . The merely
> spectacular is a disguise and a defense; it is a disguise for
> the fact that there is emptiness underneath; it is a defense
> against real awareness . . . Dostoevski was right in his
> Grand Inquisitor scene – we do not altogether want
> freedom.

More recently the philosopher John Francis Kavanaugh
expanded this line of thinking in his challenging study of
American values, *Following Christ in a Consumer Society*. His
thesis is put bluntly: 'Our problem is idolatry. Its presence
is systemic.' Later he elaborates:

> We take for granted that technical intelligence is some
> grand historic leap forward in humanity's ongoing rush

to perfection. And we do not even suspect that such an imperialism of object-knowledge over our consciousness might be related to the rise of advanced industrial capitalism and the enthronement of the commodity as the center of our lives. [This dominance by consumer commodities] is a concerted and systematic rejection of *human freedom*. By freedom I mean the human potentiality for self-commitment . . . We do not walk in freedom, since we are paralyzed by what is.

In a more recent article Kavanaugh sums up the collision between American social assumptions and the vision of the gospel:

The professed and lived values of the culture – success, power, prestige, nationalist and personal and class pride, riches and self-aggrandizement – clash so extensively and profoundly with the values of Jesus, that the follower of Christ can only experience culture as assault upon religious belief.

Jacques Ellul is the author of at least twenty books, most of which focus on the fate of faith in a technological age and on the strategies of 'the system' in forcing mankind to conform to its ways. Many of his claims are controversial and are expressed with vehemence:

Spiritually the most destructive and deceptive act is that of making a virtue of necessity . . . In the most advanced modern societies man is essentially alienated . . . To be alienated means to be someone other than oneself; it also can mean to belong to someone else . . . [This alienated self] is very busy but he is emotionally empty . . . In no other civilization has man been so totally repressed . . . The human being is no longer in any sense the agent of choice . . . We must do an iconoclastic work, destroying the false gods of our society.

The reader is invited to think through these critiques and to put flesh on them from his or her own horizon. The aim as always in these pages is to bother to be free and to realize the differentness of vision that faith entails in contemporary society.

Step 3

Escaping from the Wrong Question

I do not seek to understand in order to believe. I shall not understand unless I believe. St Anselm

Going over from the pursuit of certainty to the pursuit of understanding can be a change of mind as well as a change of heart.
John S. Dunne

In those war-time escape stories sometimes a lot of energy went in the wrong direction, at least initially. People could spend days and even weeks digging a tunnel only to find it led into a stream, which flooded and ruined their whole enterprise. In a similar way people asking about faith can waste their energies by expecting a certainty that is simply unavailable. It is like the oft-told tale of a tourist lost in the wilds of Kerry, who wanted to get back to Dublin in a hurry. He stopped his car to ask a farmer for directions, only to get the advice – 'If you want to get to Dublin, you wouldn't start from here.' There are also false starting points for the journey of faith. Due to the modern explosion of science and technology, our whole culture is 'sold' on an empirical way of knowing and seems to forget that other kinds of truth need other approach roads.

Having spent nearly twenty years in university teaching, I think the most frequent religious question I heard from students was some version of 'How can you be so sure about God?' 'Perhaps you can't,' I always replied. And I went on to admit that for me faith is a fragile kind of knowing, its 'certainty' always mixed up with 'darkness' (as Vatican I insisted). 'It would be marvellous', the students would say, 'to have some totally convincing evidence for God.' 'But that is not "on" ', I insisted. 'You are looking for the kind of certainty that would mean that faith would be no longer faith. There is no such infallible key to God. If you insist on working out his existence by "pure reason", I cannot say that you have no hope of ever arriving. But it is a rare road. More likely you are falling into the trap of equating the real with the visible, and if so you may bring a somewhat childish "show me" to the search for God. That would be imprisonment in the wrong question.'

Are there no 'proofs' then for the existence of God? I find that question difficult. Personally I hold that the traditional proofs can make sense when I am not 'God-proof', that is, locked in a wrong disposition. But I would prefer to avoid the word 'proof' as suggesting something far too mathematical: there is no way of proving the existence of God as one would verify some scientific hypothesis. That way of thinking is rooted in a false objectivity, where arriving at truth starts from taking a good hard look at the data. God remains unseen: so there can be no direct data to be examined in that way.

What I am getting at is very simple: we will never get anywhere with religious questions, until we realize that they belong to a personal region of truth, and that to face the question of God will involve the whole self. With this kind of search one cannot stand outside in a neutral fashion. Just as stained-glass windows cannot be viewed from outside the building, truth about God can never be grasped from an external perspective. It needs a logic of its own.

A true story may help to flesh out this different logic. I remember directing a retreat in a seminary some time back, when a particular student came to talk about some issues in his own life – and it was a real freedom for him to be able to speak of these personal worries for the first time. He came back the next day with quite different questions, saying that he seemed unable to pray and was wondering what faith is. I asked him whether he remembered our conversation of the previous morning. He replied that he could hardly forget and that it had been important for him in many ways. I then 'pushed' him somewhat: how did he know that I did not 'blab' about his personal life with my fellow retreat directors over dinner? No, he said, he was sure that I had never mentioned anything of what he had spoken about. But he had not had the dining room bugged: he had no idea what I had been talking about over the meal. Still, he answered, he remained certain that I had said nothing about him. 'But you have no proof of that,' I countered. 'None,' he replied, 'except that I trust you.' 'Thank you,' I remember saying, 'that is an act of faith.' That is what faith is like: not having the room bugged, but someting akin to trust between persons. The model of faith-knowledge is not verifiable knowing but inter-personal knowing. It is more akin to the mutual dependence of friends than to the detached objectivity of the natural sciences. To say this does not imply that the whole business of faith is merely subjective. But it does mean that religious truth will be found along some other road than the road of impersonal investigation.

FROM GEOMETRY TO WONDER

> Smugness is the first reward
> befalls impatient certainty –
> your world and you are in accord
> of mutual unreality
> at rest; the last is being bored.
> > R. P. Blackmur

What I have been saying so far may seem rather negative. In my own way I have been echoing what Pascal said centuries ago. Although a mathematician himself, he insisted that the 'geometric' approach could never arrive at religious reality; it might be able to acknowledge a First Cause, but it could not reach faith in the biblical God who entered into relationship with people. Which could you possibly pray to – a First Cause or the God of Abraham? Thus Pascal came to his famous conclusion that in matters of faith 'the heart has its reasons of which the reason knows nothing'. The word 'heart' in this context points to something central to humanity, not simply a matter of emotions but rather the core of a person's existence. Our problem becomes: how to escape from expecting an impossible certainty, and more posi-tively, how to find genuine 'reasons of the heart'.

For this positive search the role of imagination is crucial and yet often overlooked in talking about faith. To seek for religious truth needs something of the same imaginative receptivity as poetry. Let me illustrate what I mean by recalling an annual event in my university teaching. I often enjoyed taking an 'introduction to literature' course for first-year students, and at some stage I would write three strange sounds on the board:

HA   AHA   AH . . .

I liked to tease my audience by claiming that here we had not only three approaches to literature but three basic attitudes to human existence! It is possible to go around saying 'ha' to everything – in other words judging all the time. It is part of the study of literature to learn to evaluate, but, as in life, it is dangerous to jump to judgement: do that and you get stuck in your prejudices. I then explained how university work concentrated on 'aha' – pronounced with a rising rhythm – to express the moment of understanding or intellectual discovery. A degree course should offer a feast of 'aha' by exploring many new angles of insight into literature. But beware, I would solemnly say to those assembled first-year students, of the excitement of 'aha' suppressing something even more basic – the 'ah' experience, the level of wonder that poetry requires if it is to be received in its richness. The object of my three primitive sounds was to warn the innocent beginner that the 'ah' experience cannot be taught. Universities specialize in insights (aha) and in judgements (ha); they can often neglect what is central and deepest (ah . . .).

What professional study can do with literature, our whole culture can do with the question of faith. Indeed in university circles it is not unusual to find embarrassed immaturity over religious issues. Church religion is often dismissed in a spirit of 'ha' – a jumping to judgement that lacks real experiencing or understanding. Or the ancient questions of faith can be avoided in a spirit of 'aha' – if there is no provable truth, the whole thing must be a private affair, like taste in music. Once again the forgotten foundation stone is 'ah . . .' A religious journey must begin with some experience of wonder; otherwise one will neither be in touch with one's deepest hungers nor able to listen to the love poetry of God which is called revelation. Understanding and judgement are essential on the road to the 'yes' of faith but they are not the starting point.

Unless this is grasped, I can be deceived into thinking that faith is like other kinds of knowledge. It is more like poetry than like physics; it asks that I open a door within myself that is not a door of pure reason.

Wallace Stevens (himself one of the great agnostic poets of this century) once remarked that 'the purely realistic mind never experiences any passion for reality'. His 'realistic' mind refers to someone caught in the limited world of outer knowing, and so unable to enter into the 'ah . . .' experience. To be like that means neglecting part of our humanity. In this respect, a psychologist friend of mine has been outlining to me some well-known theories of the brain, and applying them to his own religious difficulties. It seems that the right hemisphere of our cerebral cortex differs from the left. They have significantly different functions to perform: the left specializes in logical analysis of information, whereas the right side is more creative and intuitive, gathering our experiences into patterns and unities. Thus where the left deals with language skills, the right allows for the appreciation of music. This friend of mine would like to believe in God – and this hope of his belongs on the right side of the brain with its capacity for harmony. But this desire is often brow-beaten, so to speak, by his psychological training and the scepticism cultivated on the left side of his brain. It is not untypical of our educated world that the analytical self can frighten and frustrate the intuitive self in this way. If so, the road to religious faith is blocked, and until 'pure reason' is dethroned from its dicatorship, there will be a stunting of the 'ah . . .' dimension and of the 'reasons of the heart'. Dominance by the left brain cramps our human possibilities; it spells the death of wonder and of imagination as roads of truth.

After this chapter had been drafted, I received a letter from the friend I have been mentioning here, in which he records some of his own change of focus:

> 'Up till now I believed that empiricism was the only way of arriving at truth and that nothing else was reliable. Discussing all this with a Jewish student, he asked me a key question: 'How would I know truth if I saw it?'
>
> I always thought that truth was something we could never quite reach and that it wasn't our destiny to find

it. I never realized that my system actually excluded the possibility of truth.

That is as good a statement as I know of the limitations of one-dimensional thinking, which equates knowing with taking-a-good-look-at-external-data. But there are other levels of truth and other avenues towards apprehending them.

IMAGINATIVE FAITH

The imagination is the ordinary mind in an extraordinary phase, far beyond its predicted course. Denis Donoghue

The imagination is really the only way we have of handling the world. William Lynch

Can imagination claim to reach truth? Perhaps it is the ally we need in order to escape finally from the wrong question and from the wrong emphasis in any search for God. Of course many people confuse the imaginative with the imaginary: faith can be imaginative (rooted in its own language of images) without being imaginary (a product of fantasy and therefore false). I think imagination has been badly neglected by theologians as they pondered the nature of faith. Thomas Aquinas, for instance, is marvellously lucid in pinpointing how faith-knowing differs from other kinds of knowledge: he calls it an act of the intellect commanded by the will. In other words, it is an unusual kind of truth because decision plays a crucial role along the way to saying 'yes'. I would want to propose 'imagination' as an equal partner with 'intellect' and 'will' in the whole business of faith. 'Intellect' is practically the same as what I was calling 'aha'. 'Will' is close to 'ha'. What is imagination then except the source of the 'ah . . .' experience? It is our capacity to think by means of stories and metaphors. In fact, stories and metaphors are the most adequate vehicles we have for approaching God, and to judge from the imaginative richness of the Bible itself, they are also the language God uses for approaching us. Is this not what Newman had in mind when he claimed that 'the heart is commonly reached, not through the reason, but through the imagination'?

I have been insisting on the uniqueness of the knowledge that we call faith. It has its roots more in 'heart' and 'imagination' and right-side brain than in 'reason' and 'verification' and left-side brain. We started from the question whether we could be sure about faith. My answer is a version of 'yes, but'. I see faith as a non-rational and personal kind of truth – but it is not irrational. Reasons can be given to support a decision of faith, but they never add up to a water-tight proof. In this sense the evidence for God is always incomplete or indirect, and so it is never able to satisfy our longing for conclusiveness.

To expect some conclusive argument about God is a false hope: that all-or-nothing mentality never fits the deeper human questions. But I find it hard to exorcize that hope – even in myself. I find a constant temptation to fall into the 'funk hole of objectivity', as Harry Williams has called it. Faith is a knowledge where disposition makes all the difference. It is a road that differs from all our normal knowing. That is why it can seem so fragile whenever the 'realistic mind' is in control. I have to escape from such realism in order to find reality.

And in recent years some exciting rebellions are taking place against the rationalisms that have ruled our lives. I am thinking of those new movements that seek to rescue us from a male dominance in all things. Feminism for me has stopped being a matter of women's rights alone: it is part of a new consciousness about women and men alike. Many of the new 'spiritualities' invite us to renew our trust in the more maternal sides of our humanity: encouraging the 'child' to find expression, owning our feelings, fostering the artist in each person, cherishing the physical body and the whole cosmos. But this kind of talk seems 'soft' to the 'man-made' culture all around us. It is no coincidence that within this same culture faith has been despised as an unprovable and unproductive wisdom.

For some centuries now, reason of the verification-efficiency variety has held increasing sway. It has created a culture that ignores and suppresses the religious imagination, with the result that faith seems more and more like a poor relation. Poetry, intuition, story-telling – within the house of truth, all these have been banished to the basement. They are dismissed as secondary to the central compulsions of market efficiency and aggressive politics. Thus another Cinderella sits beside the kitchen fire and other ugly sisters rule the roost; jealous of her beauty, they laugh at her poor attire. But another fairy godmother has begun to arrive through that new consciousness I touched upon. It rejects not technology in itself but the monopoly of that one mentality over so much that calls for a different human wavelength. To rediscover the human becomes the goal of many progressive people today. It means refusing to equate truth with external objectivity. It means accepting anew the differentness of religious truth and recognizing again, but as inhabitants of our time, the perennial strangeness of faith.

SCAFFOLDING FOR REFLECTION

These are some quotations for the reader to wrestle with, in the hope that they may invite him or her into further pondering the nature of the faith question:

> It is the peculiar and unique nature of ultimate truth to demand the collaboration of reason and imagination: the isolated intellect alone cannot find it.   (Richard Kroner)

> We have tested and tasted too much, lover –
> Through a chink too wide there comes in no wonder.
>
> . . . . .
>
> And I have a feeling
> That through the hole in reason's ceiling
> We can fly to knowledge
> Without ever going to college.
> (Patrick Kavanagh – from 'Advent' and 'To Hell
> with Commonsense')

> If a man does nothing more than argue, if he has nothing deeper at bottom, if he does not seek God by some truer means . . . by faith prior to demonstrations, he will either not attain truth or attain a shallow, unreal view of it.
> (J. H. Newman, writing in 1838)

> I would rather have a crumb of real truth, however starved

I felt, than a whole loaf of half-truth . . . I feel there must
be truths which are true in the spiritual sphere but which
cannot be exactly correlated with the 'truths' of ordinary
knowledge and that much misery and self-torture has arisen
from a confusion between the functions of the two.

(Antonia White)

A materialist scientist is like a man who, although in
possession of a radio receiver, refuses to use it because he
has made up his mind that nothing but atmospheric noises
can be obtained from it.   (E. F. Schumacher)

God does not form part of our common experience. God is
not a fact, any more than he is an 'object'. The reality of
God is not that of an event . . . God is unique.

(Henri de Lubac)

In that faith is more than any establishable synthesis of
reason (seen as knowledge), in that it is an act of the whole
living human being and not merely the exercising of one of
his functions (that is, the function of reason), it is therefore
basically both impossible and indeed contradictory that
faith's content (which is God freely revealing himself)
should be 'proved' or that faith as an act (man responding
freely to God) should be elicited from man as some logically
necessary response . . . The decisive factor in the fact of
faith is taking the risk of surrendering ourselves to the
freedom of love of God.   (Hans Urs von Balthasar)

The matter is essentially a simple one: empty society of
the experience of shared value and commitment, exclude
wonder and reverence as legitimate human responses to
the world, isolate men and women within the trap of their
own limited and limiting goals, and they will cease to speak
of God . . . If there is any truth at all in the idea that we
live in an age of *doubt*, it lies not in the advance of knowledge, but in the impoverishment of our collective percep-
tions, in the emptying of our language and our society of
anything but number and calculation.   (Eamon Duffy)

Step 4

Escaping from Strange Gods

While in other sciences the instruments you use are things external to yourself (things like microscopes and telescopes), the instrument through which you see God is your whole self. And if a man's self is not kept clean and bright, his glimpse of God will be blurred – like the Moon seen through a dirty telescope. C. S. Lewis

Over the years I have listened a lot to students, and that listening has taught me reverence for the many struggles that go on within young people. If I were asked to sum up what were the most frequent areas of searching, I would have no difficulty in singling out two in particular: problems of self-worth and problems over images of God. The issues often seemed connected and to arise in that order. First, someone would want to express something of his or her own personal experience, and only then would the question expand into more spiritual or religious areas. Looking back I am struck by how seldom an explicitly religious question was the starting point. Nearly always the first step beyond talk about academic work had to do with some hidden and negative feelings: loneliness, anxiety, family conflict, relationships, bereavement. Often there was a lot of self-doubt lurking behind the officially successful university student. Usually there had been little or no previous opportunity to express emotions or explore where 'one was at'. And always I found that the listening and the speaking would unearth a 'hidden treasure' in gospel terms, the good news behind the bad, the true self emerging from the false. An earlier section here elaborated on that first essential escape into self-freedom. We now turn to the second major issue – trying to purify the picture of 'God'.

It is right to put that three-letter word in quotes because

just as there are many versions of a true and false self, so
there are many kinds of true and false 'God'. Central to this
book is the thesis that faith becomes more possible when a
four-fold escape story is enacted – escaping not only from the
false to the true self, not only from being the victim of a
twisted system or being caught within the wrong question,
but also finding ways to escape from the false gods to the true
God. It is possible to be imprisoned within more than one
kind of falsity at once: I have known people to go round in
frustrating circles when, for instance, their hurt or fearful self
kept rejecting a cold or cruel 'God'. Unless the agenda can
be changed, the outcome can only be negative. Often I found
myself saying, as is reported of the early Christians, 'but I
too am an atheist of that kind of god'.

One of the most vivid images of a false god that I can
remember came from the lips of a young Dubliner who was
preparing for his marriage in church. When I asked him if
he believed in God, he answered with a certain casualness.
'Oh sure – someone must have made all this.' In my own
mind I wondered whether this view was any advance on
deism – that uninvolved acknowledgement of a First Cause.
So I asked David if he thought this 'god' would be for him
or against him. 'He'd be a bit against me I think. I've done
a few things in my time.' Had he any picture of this somewhat
hostile divinity? Like a flash came a marvellous reply: 'I think
of him with a telescope.' This image captures the core of
David's false god: far away, stern in judgement, and ultimately a Spy. After some perusing of the gospels together, it
was not too difficult a transition for David to let go of this
impoverished image and begin to glimpse the God of Christian revelation. To put words on such strange gods is often
to banish them, even to exorcise them through laughter.

I recall a priest who, in the course of making a retreat,
found another false god lurking within him. During his few
days of quiet he met with me once a day to reflect on how
the inner journey was going. On the first day he remarked,
half-amused, half-serious, but with a certain self-impatience,
'I think God should give me a good kick.' When he repeated
the same comment twice the following day, I asked him,
'Would Jesus give you a good kick?' 'Oh no' was his somewhat
shocked reply. 'So for you Jesus is not God?' I inquired. 'Of

course he is,' and he laughed, embarrassed by his latent heresy. His image of 'God' was judgemental and punitive but the image of God in Jesus allowed him to escape this more childish and fearful 'God'. Even in those who are aware of the true God intellectually, such a dichotomy is surprisingly common: their hearts and feelings and spontaneous reactions have not caught up with the truth of their minds. The (childish) child is not only father but master of the man.

Many of these negative images can be hangovers from the sensitivities of early years. In fact that priest had known a strict upbringing from parents who believed in the 'good kick' of corporal punishment, and David's early experience of his family was one of non-communication and lack of warmth. There were obviously links between such shaping experiences and their distorted pictures of God. I know others whose God of Impossible Standards had his origin in 'loving' but manipulative parents (especially mothers, it must be said). Where home games of Mummy-won't-be-pleased or Mummy-must-always-be-pleased form the hidden agenda of childhood, a message sinks in that Only the Ideal is Acceptable – but the ideal turns out to be impossible. Therefore life becomes a futile quest to be approved and God becomes the Great Displeased, the One with the Frown and the Pointing Finger.

Other impoverished images stem from what is communicated to (or at least received by) the young child through school or church. I am amazed at how often some threatening remark about God can linger long in the memory. Something like, 'if you are telling lies about those sweets, you can't fool God – he will know everything,' may prove deeply disturbing to a young child. And the image born in such moments is not easily wiped out by doctrines learned later about a God of love. Probably the damage can only be undone by some positive contrary experience.

A PROCESSION OF IDOLS

There is nothing so dangerous as religion. It can congeal into legalism and ritualism. Walter Kasper

Saying good-bye to one kind of sub-Christian God will be part of the process. Robert Butterworth

Because more than half the battle in escaping from these strange gods is to identify them, the remainder of this section will simply list several of the more frequent false images that I have discovered in myself and in others over the years, offering only a brief comment on each.

Perhaps most subtle but frequently unacknowledged is the Invisible Super-Power who is Out-There-Somehow. United in this global image are three sub-images: the god of explanations, who remains a vague but distant force, and with whom relationship seems impossible. This is a god who fades fast and becomes redundant when somebody takes responsibility for his or her own humanity: it is the watchmaker model rejected as an unnecessary hypothesis by modern humanism. The true God of Revelation is indeed beyond us, transcendent and almighty, but the whole thrust of the biblical drama is to show him with us in history, within us as Spirit, becoming one of us in humanity, and in a sense powerless through love for us. As with all these false images, the man-made god can lurk in a person's consciousness as a distorting mirror and so block any 'coming and seeing' of the God-given God.

Tennyson once said that 'the general English view of God is as an immeasurable clergyman'. This God of the Institution seems to epitomize the foibles and failings of his official representatives: bossy, cranky, moody, peevish, fussy, petty, stuffy, petulant ... all multiplied by infinity! He is also Someone who likes what we never like, the frequently awful language of church rituals (awful in the modern usage while seeking to be awe-full in the older sense).

A more crude variation is the Solemn Bore. One can instance those off-putting and legalistic conversations of the Trinity in Milton's *Paradise Lost*. If he is so pompous in himself, he becomes something of a spoilsport for us, like a difficult grandfather in whose presence the children must stop making noise.

From a child's perspective the Bore easily slides over into the Big Bully and, even worse, into the Torturer God, who is the summary of all childhood nightmares and horror stories. Images of hell run deep in people's primitive selves. I think of Gerard Hughes' marvellous parable of Uncle George in his *God of Surprises:* a little child is taken on a tour of his uncle's huge mansion and shown a dungeon of flames and punishment, only to be told that this will be his lot if he does not come to visit Uncle George regularly from now on.

Of course the vengeful or punitive god need not wait until the next life. Many people seem to think of him as planning a downfall for them here and therefore interpret any accident or tragedy as punishment for wrongdoing. This can go hand-in-hand with singing 'The Lord is my Shepherd' and meaning it, but when disaster strikes that pastoral image can easily give way to the god-who-cannot-be-trusted – although it might not be expressed in so many words.

Perhaps childhood is responsible for yet another silly but understandable picture – the God of Magic Interference. Influenced by the many overly visual portrayals of the supernatural in film or television, this is an image of the spectacular miracle-worker – often involving events of a showy but fruitless kind. On more adult reflection this god comes under fire. Why does he show off his powers in such a selective way? Why does he not interfere to prevent so much human suffering? Behind what can seem a plausible 'force' for good (as in *Star Wars*) there lurks an image of a god of favourites and ultimately of disinterest in ordinary human struggles. Thus he becomes, as with all these false images, a god not worth believing in.

Akin to this is the God-Who-Didn't-Give-What-I-Asked. Here we have a more personal approach to the Super-Power God, except that now he is a source of disillusionment. This is the reverse of the Impossible Standards God, because now he is to be manipulated into agreeing with our wisdom. But he fails to live up to our expectations or to co-operate with our plans. Put like that the cheapness of this image becomes apparent. It is another face of the Security-Blanket God as encountered in American religious television. The idea implicit here is what one Latin American commentary has called a 'paternalistic God who leaves everything readymade'.

Finally, it is easy to suspect God of being a Jealous Competitor for our attention. In this view he remains a difficult Outsider-to-Life who is forever demanding that we remember him and who becomes sulky when we immerse ourselves in reality.

ESCAPE FROM IMMATURITY

> *God made his appearance in religion under the frigid title of the First Cause, and was appropriately worshipped in whitewashed churches.* A. N. Whitehead

If God were to take a libel action against humanity, what defence could be offered for such reductive and distorted portrayals? No doubt a skilful defence lawyer could argue that the Bible itself lends support to some of these images. But we shall see later on (in our 'Love Stories' section) that the core of Christian revelations is of a God undreamed of in these blinkered and frightening pictures. Why then are strange gods so common in human consciousness? The only valid defence must lie in the poverty of our language and of our level of receiving revelation.

On reflection many of those false images arise from an encounter between the impressionable imagination of childhood and the rougher edges of religion. If there are no opportunities for healing these experiences, an adult can later get stuck with a god unworthy of his or her humanity and even more unworthy of the God of Jesus Christ. Nor can Christianity as lived absolve itself from blame: we have never been immune from distortion and narrowing of the vision entrusted to us. Thus the all-too-human face of church religion has rightly been the target of critique from both believers and unbelievers alike. One thinks of Dostoevsky's Grand Inquisitor, the embodiment of all that is worst in church control, announcing to Jesus himself: 'We have corrected your great work and have founded it on *miracle, mystery and authority*.' In his view humanity proved too weak and cowardly to reach for the frightening freedom of Jesus.

The great atheists also can be looked on as all too accurately diagnosing the impoverished forms of Christianity. Perhaps this can best be illustrated from what has been termed 'the school of suspicion'. They accuse religion of being a mere crutch, the projection of a 'dream' born from human weakness (Feuerbach). Or they dismiss it as social escapism, understandable because the 'oppressed creature' within a 'heartless world' needs some solace (Marx). Again it is judged to be a psychological compensation that offers 'illusion' in order to cope with the tragedies of life (Freud). These three voices and others not only unmask the complacent tendencies of religion but serve to purify immature images of God and to throw one back to the full story of the Scriptures.

This problem of images can be linked with the larger crisis of institutions that is part of contemporary culture. It would seem that in a more stable world many people survived with their faith intact in spite of some immature and false images. But in a period of such mobility, a more internalized faith will be needed, and hence the images of God have to be genuine to be accepted at all. Some research by James Fowler can offer light here (as well as pointing us more positively towards our 'quest stories'). Fowler has specialised in studies of 'faith development' and he sees the language of faith as naturally expanding through the phases of each individual lifespan. While this is not the moment to enter into the full scope of his 'stages of faith', one particular transition seems relevant to the question of images of God. Fowler argues that most religious institutions have been more comfortable when people stay within a church-reliant faith rather than progress to the normal adult language of faith-as-decision. The less mature of those two stages is happier accepting authority from outside the self. The more adult faith-language goes beyond this conventional belonging to a more explicit commitment to God and an ability to live religious values even in a hostile environment.

In this perspective many of our false images of God seem to originate in immaturities of one kind or another. Many of them, as we have seen, can be transferences from childhood vulnerability. Others also start from assumptions of inferiority: for instance, where 'God' is hostile and judgemental, or where he seems the arbitrary and uncaring shaper of one's destiny. Another set of false images stems from a naive 'geography', a visual thinking which locates God as Outsider Up-There-Somewhere. Escaping from these imprisoning images means escaping from the latent immaturity that plagues us all. It means getting beyond magic and into genuine mystery. Magic offers childish ways of controlling the incomprehensible. Mystery invites us to acknowledge, not that something cannot be understood, but rather that it is too rich for mere understanding. Mystery calls for reverence

and a spirit of true worship. The false images need no rever-
ence and no real worship. And so, as the poet Patrick
Kavanagh put it, 'God unworshipped withers to the Futile
One.'

SCAFFOLDING FOR REFLECTION

This time we draw on a book first published in 1960 by the
theologian Henri de Lubac. Entitled *The Discovery of God*, it
is one of the most profound and meditative books I know in
this whole area.

> We have witnessed, during the last few centuries, 'the
> rationalist evaporation of God'. But it was the rationalist
> God. A single puff will disperse the vapour. We shall not
> be disturbed. We shall even breathe more comfortably. The
> true God, the God we continue to adore, is elsewhere.

> Whenever it abandons a system of thought, humanity
> imagines it has lost God . . . Industrial civilisations are
> naturally atheistic, and agricultural civilisations are
> naturally pagan. Faith in the true God is always a victory.

> It is possible to maintain that religion – faith in God in the
> first instance – is a system invented by nature with the
> object of *reassuring* man who would otherwise be paralysed
> by fear in face of a hostile mystery . . . Faith, indeed,
> reassures us – but not on our level, or so as to produce a
> paralysing illusion, or a complacent satisfaction, but so as
> to enable us to act. It gives man the confidence to become
> worthy of himself.

A more recent book by Juan Arias, *The God I Don't Believe
In*, ends with a litany of the many false faces of God. Inspired
by his example I offer here my own adaptation of some of
those idols:

> the god who pounces on sinners;
> the god who doesn't need humanity;
> the god who doesn't care about Calcutta;
> the god who despises human happiness;
> the god who says, 'you will pay for that';

the god who has no emotions;
the god who is a specialist in souls;
the god who would only reluctantly become a man . . .

and Arias ends – 'Yes my God is the other God.'

Finally, the reader may find food for thought in this passage from a pastoral letter issued by the Irish Catholic Bishops to mark International Year of Youth in 1985:

> Some people carry around with them an image of God that is in fact superstitious. It is the image of the punishing puppet-master who has to be humoured and pacified in case he might pull the wrong string. Others picture him as a distant, inaccessable authority figure who is totally out of tune with the friendship held out to us in Christ. A surprising number of people look on God as a kind of clock-maker – a God of explanation for the universe but a God irrelevant to ordinary life. There are even those who only know him as a God of the gaps. He has no compelling existence until favours are needed or trouble strikes.

That pastoral continues by evoking the contrary image of the Christian God – in a few strong sentences that point towards our later 'Love Stories' section:

> The only God worth believing in is the God who believed enough in people to die for us. The only God worth living for is the One who calls us to live with him, through dark faith in this life, and beyond death in face-to-face fullness. The only God worth searching for is the One who searched for us and who still struggles within us in order that we may become more free to love.

CONVERGENCE OF ESCAPE STORIES

Not all our actions of each day or of our whole life proceed from our liberty . . . Liberty is not ready-made. Juan Luis Segundo

The novelist Iris Murdoch has accused the modern world of falling into a facile and 'consoling dream', through forgetting that freedom means an uphill climb. All our chapters so far

to counteract that innocence, by suggesting four
wakening into pre-faith freedoms.

... ...undation stone of this 'escape' section was quite
simple: it argued that to approach Christian faith solely in
terms of truth is to put the cart before the horse. There is a
prior struggle of self freedom.

Imagine the somewhat extreme situation in which a person
falls victim to all four falsities, as we have been outlining
them. He or she would be imprisoned in the desolations of
the false self, would be kidnapped within a false set of social
values, would try to approach religious truth from an impossible angle, and would be handicapped by inadequate images
of God. That is simply a formula for religious impotence. But
the opposite situation can come about through a four-fold
struggle to escape.

(1)   Any reflective atheist that I have known would agree
that our culture can imprison us in impoverished layers of
consciousness. So the inner self needs to learn to listen to
reality – through skills of stillness and discernment.

(2)   In the context of dehumanizing pressures and the unjust
divisions of our planet, interior life is not enough. We need
not only to mock the system but to resist it – through skills
of social critique and the creation of alternative lifestyles.

(3)   Much arguing over religion is naive, because blinkered
versions of truth hold sway. We need an expansion of what
we mean by knowledge – through skills of intelligent wonder
and imagination.

(4)   To fight false gods is a waste of energy. We need to
exorcize those childish deities – through skills of scripture,
through dialogue with others about faith or unfaith, and
ultimately through the transformation that is prayer.

Our journey so far might be captured in a saying much
liked by Matthew Arnold: 'Firstly, never go against the best
light you have: secondly, take care that your light be not
darkness.'

Part 2

Quest Stories

Twenty years ago a book on faith would plunge straight into the topic of this section: are there good reasons for believing in God? The logic behind this book demanded that we spend time preparing the way for such questions. The reason is not that modern culture is openly hostile to faith, but rather that it silently ignores religious questions and can induce a certain despair about the possibility of tackling them intelligently. So our first two sections faced four forms of possible imprisonment. We needed skills of both contemplation and critique before coming to the issue of the credibility of faith in God. We also needed to sift out true from false approaches to questions of faith and to discern true from false images of God.

All that was preparatory work, because to start from unfreedom would mean a fruitless journey. But it is possible to clear the ground for a garden, removing rocks and rubbish, and yet to sow no seeds and grow no flowers. This part of the book is the time for planting: the aim now is to offer a map towards faith, a set of four 'quest stories'.

To look for something that is missing is one of the recurring plots in all literature. One could interpret Hamlet's central obsession as a search for certainty. The typical pattern of all thrillers is a quest for who-done-it. It has been my experience that most people, if they write poetry, do so from some sense of lostness rather than of light. In short, the 'quest story' is a basic experience.

Here we are going to look at four great avenues of questing for God. Each starts from something fundamental in humanity. Together they form a powerful argument towards the possibility of faith, but it is a logic of the whole person, an existential logic. They are not proofs but pointers. They are not syllogisms but stories. They do not carry us to faith itself but only to a threshold of hearing from which faith might be born.

Step 5

The Heart's Hunger

From early on we are searching. All we do is crave, cry out. Do not have what we want. Ernst Bloch

Man has little needs and deeper needs. We have fallen into the mistake of living from our little needs till we have almost lost our deeper needs in a sort of madness. D. H. Lawrence

Our first road will be that of St Augustine, whose journey towards faith was marked by so much turmoil within himself, His temperament is summed up in those famous words which come on the first page of his Confessions: 'You have made us for yourself and our hearts are restless until they find their rest in you.' His whole book tells of the adventure of his heart's hunger, and of the many evasions that he went through before being able to recognize Christ as God. Even then it meant another costly step to let go of his life of pleasure and to surrender his whole self in the yes of faith. His story tells of a desperate search for fulfilment in false directions, which left him with a strong sense of the relativity of all pleasures and achievements. He was a passionate man of deep desires, but caught in what he came to call 'a fugitive's freedom'. As he said in a memorable phrase, 'There I was going mad on the way to sanity.'

The gnawing frustration of Augustine's life lay in a sense of not having discovered what he was born for. He knew that he could never feel totally at home in the world. But why such longing? When I have so much to satisfy me, why all this restless desire within me? Where to find lasting peace? How to shake off this nagging sense of falsity and incompleteness? These were some of the questions that served as a trigger for the Augustine journey to faith. He came to interpret his experience as a kind of homesickness and of God-intended 'holy longing'. What had trapped him in negativity and impotence for so long? 'If we love, we see.' His heart had been in self-turmoil all these years when it thought it was searching honestly and openly. The key to Augustine's escape story lay in a new listening to love and then a new seeing in love.

Our argument here is very simple; Augustine is only the headline. Something of the same restlessness is felt in different ways by many people and it can be one of the most fruitful pointers towards faith. One of Saul Bellow's characters, Henderson the Rain King, had a voice inside him that continually said, 'I want, I want'; but it would never tell him what it wanted! How am I to get in touch with my deeper desires, in order to listen to them and to live more fully from them? Another of Bellow's characters voices an answer: there are two great awakeners of the spirit from its sleep – love and suffering. I think many people start their version of the Augustine journey from the collapse of complacency and routine: some crisis or pain becomes the awakening to the submerged restlessness that was always there. Then the great hungers of the heart insist on being heard. When it is painfully obvious that I am not my own goal, the question arises; have I any goal at all? Why this frustrated and frustrating longing to reach beyond my limited self? Can the questions of Yeats find any answer?

> But is there any comfort to be found?
> Man is in love and loves what vanishes,
> What more is there to say?

At first what is being evoked here must seem negative – an emptiness, a level of thirst that is never met by 'passing things'. But what is this experience saying? Where is it pointing? Having lived with his turmoils and his hungers for a long time, Augustine at last came to the famous and eloquent answer, as expressed in his Confessions: 'You were with me but I was not with you'; he had been 'in love with loving' so much that he had missed noticing the Lover. I believe that the Augustine road is a familiar one to many in search of meaning and faith today. It is not a matter of repeating his particular emotions or patterns of experience. Rather it is a

matter of being in touch with one's cluster of heart-hungers
and of trusting them as pointers towards God.

Our Yeats quotation is just one of hundreds that could
be gathered from poetry through the centuries, because the
transience of happiness is one of the perennial themes of
literature. We seldom 'find in ourselves alone enough supplies
to last the winter' of existence (a memorable phrase from
Hans Urs von Balthasar). What are such images saying to
us? That life is ultimately unsatisfying and that is the whole
story? Or that life is ultimately unsatisfying and that is not
the whole story? That second response has been true for many
people through the ages who found their own emptiness to
be a pulley towards another vision altogether. This whole
approach has seldom been captured with more delightful
clarity than in a poem by George Herbert entitled 'The
Pulley', where he imagines God as giving every blessing to
humanity except one:

> When God at first made man,
> Having a glass of blessings standing by,
> Let us (said he) pour on him all we can;
> Let the world's riches, which dispersed lie,
>   Contract into a span.
>
> So strength first made a way,
> Then beauty flow'd, then wisdom, honour, pleasure:
> When almost all was out, God made a stay,
> Perceiving that alone of all his treasure
>   Rest on the bottom lay.

At his point, God stops to ponder the consequence of letting
humanity have this 'jewel' of being totally at home in the
world. He decides to keep this one gift ungiven, for fear that
if they become totally satisfied with life, mankind might lose
any longing to know God. So Herbert's final stanza begins
with a pun:

> Yet let him keep the rest,
> But keep them with repining restlessness:
> Let him be rich and weary, that at least,
> If goodness lead him not, yet weariness
>   May toss him to my breast.

Those last lines are a marvellous summary of what is being suggested in this section – that the absence of lasting 'rest', even in a 'rich' existence, often serves as a starting point for a journey towards faith. This is not an argument for the mind; it is an experience of strange 'weariness' or 'restlessness' of heart. It would be ridiculous to claim that these unfulfilled desires constitute a proof of the existence of God. Rather they create a space for wondering and for personal hunger. Such an experience often becomes a pointer towards the possibility of God. Perhaps when joined with other pointers – to be explored here – it can form an even stronger convergence, a probability.

This Augustine road is hardly an everyday phenomenon, and yet there can be few lives that do not experience something of this troubled thirst at various important moments. Sometimes this strikes at times of shock, as when some shadow of mortality falls on the complacent self. Sometimes even in the midst of great happiness, people experience a strange sense of limitation and of longing for something more lasting. It can be through moments of wordless joy – such as the birth of a child – that someone touches a certain awe and seems in contact with a sense of greatness beyond one's own self. What all such moments have in common is that self-sufficiency breaks down and unrecognized hungers are opened. This is the moment of the 'pulley', when what initially seems a burden, weighing one down, turns out to be an invitation, lifting one towards new faith-possibilities.

SCAFFOLDING FOR REFLECTION

What is proposed here is an imaginative exercise that may help the reader get in touch with his or her hunger for God. The inspiration comes from an image in a poem of religious struggle written by John Donne. Entitled 'Satire III' and composed in his youth, it makes fun of those who do not take the question of faith seriously and who waste their energies on secondary issues. Towards the close of the poem he envisages the search for truth as an uphill climb:

On a huge hill,
Cragged, and steep, Truth stands, and he that will
Reach her, about must, and about must go;
And what the hill's suddenness resists, win so.

Imagine the details of this scene. A difficult mountain with the person of Truth visible at the summit. But many obstacles and dangers. A route that proves winding and leaves you exhausted, wanting to abandon the attempt. But reaching the top is not impossible, just difficult and at times frustrating. Into that imagined struggle let the words of Jesus come, 'What do you want?' Faced with the 'hill's suddenness', when it becomes suddenly steep, have you the willingness to keep going? What keeps you climbing? Other details will suggest themselves to the reader's imagination, for instance, the beckoning figure at the top of the hill. If one is able to enter into some such fantasy, it is amazing how vivid it can become as a mode of exploration. Here it is one way of reliving something of the Augustine journey and in particular of experiencing the victory of desire over dullness within the self.

Step 6

The Wondering Mind

We can feed this mind of ours in a wise passiveness.
William Wordsworth

Jumping out of our human facts will not help at all.
William Lynch

Some eight centuries after Augustine another giant of Christian thought arrived on the scene, almost a giant in the literal sense as well. Thomas Aquinas was a huge man of a quite different style – much less passionate, more a man of quiet precision. But he shared with Augustine a long involvement with questions about faith. As a child he was so large and so silent that he was nicknamed 'Dumb Ox' by his schoolmates. It is said that he only once asked a question in class, but that question was to be the central search of his life: 'What is God?' His way of tackling that question was much more serene than the agonized Augustine, and had a different starting-point: he began less from looking inwards to his own hungers and more from looking outwards to existence itself and asking 'why'. Far from being the dunce that his family thought him to be, this youth of much silence emerged as one of the great intellects of his time, someone who when asked what gave him most gratitude before God, replied, 'I understood every page I ever read'.

But to describe Thomas in this way could give the impression of a withdrawn thinker who created a ladder of logic to God. This would be to miss the whole tone of his exploring, as rooted in a spirit of wonder about everything. His philosophy starts always from the real world and this becomes his springboard for deep reflection. About humanity in general he was more optimistic than Augustine, and always quietly confident that the human mind could arrive at certainty about God's existence. With a down-to-earth realism, he admitted that this might not be everyone's road. For most people knowledge about God would start from revelation, simply because they did not have the opportunities to ponder everything in depth. Actually his own roads to God start from something very simple – a sense that this world in itself does not explain itself. Let me recall a true story that sums up for me something of the genius of the Thomist approach. When I was studying philosophy of God under a professor who loved Aquinas, one day a fellow-student brought up the problem of evolution and asked, somewhat glibly and defiantly, what St Thomas would say to that. The reply came at once, almost with the quiet strength of the so-called Angelic Doctor: 'He would say that evolution might be a good description but it can never be an explanation. Is a rose only a collection of atoms?' That answer was an invitation to let go of cleverness and to enter a more fundamental questioning. It is one thing to understand the details of this world and how it works. It is quite different to stand back and inquire about the 'why' of existence itself. Only on that wavelength of basic wonder, and not as some piece of easy argument, can the famous 'ways' of Aquinas become pointers to God today.

The Aquinas road tries to use the human mind to the full in seeking answers to the big questions about life. But there is a deep and a surface way of tackling such questions. The surface way is to situate myself outside the issues, as if looking for some impersonal hypothesis that might explain existence. The true stance is to start from a sense of personal wonder and from that position of being grasped by the question, to seek an answer that will make a difference to my own vision of life. In short, this road requires me to experience the questions as something more than questions for 'pure reason'.

A simple exercise may illustrate the level of wonder that I am advocating as fundamental here. Hold up your hand and gaze at it for at least a minute. Move the fingers gently. Look at the strange and beautiful shape of everything. Notice the many tiny lines and the circles that are your fingerprint. Your hand is alive, unique, marvellous in its organization. Allow the sheer contemplation of your hand to lead you into realms of wonder. From that basis in wonder encourage the great questions to come forth: Is there a pattern behind existence itself? Why are we here? Why does the world exist at all? Must it have some origin and some purpose? Trying to answer these questions can lead into labyrinths of complexity. But if they are raised in the right spirit, then even pondering the questions can prove a pointer to God. Along this road, belief in God can come through savouring the quest itself. Working on the answers is a specialist business but everyone can experience the 'why' of their own existence and that of the world around.

SCAFFOLDING FOR REFLECTION

Consider the following as a modern version of the Aquinas road to God:

> If something began to exist at some time, then there must have been a cause for its existence. If something shows evidence of being planned in some way, then there must have been someone to shape that plan.

Think through those statements with some examples, which are expressed here in a deliberately simple way:

(1) If a Mummy cat has kittens, you know that there must have been a Daddy cat around some weeks ago! And yet that encounter is not the entire story. They had a major part to play in the coming-into-existence of a few kittens, and this is what the old philosophy called 'efficient causality'. But the Mummy and Daddy cats did not cause the 'nature' of cats in general. Cats did not always exist. No doubt they evolved from earlier species and those went back further, and so on. The arrival of one kitten is easily explained. The beginning of existence itself is not so easy.

(2) Imagine visiting an aeroplane plant. It is a huge place with many different sections. Everyone has a specialized work to do. But eventually out comes a new Jumbo jet and it takes off into the sky. It would be ridiculous to say that it all happened by chance.

(3) Suppose you are playing poker. If one of the players gets four aces on the first hand, you pay up and admire his 'luck'. But if he gets four aces again on the second hand, you have a hunch that such coincidences do not just happen.

Enlarge these questions to the world itself or to human life as a whole. Within themselves do they have an adequate explanation for their existence or for the rich complexity that is theirs?

Thinking along those lines s certainly a strand in the history of thinking about God. To some people it is suspect in that it could lead to a cold conclusion, a merely impersonal God. To others it is inadequate in that it does not do justice to the complexity of creation or of causality. Before ending our scaffolding section, this approach can be given a larger context by drawing upon two philosophical studies of religious belief: Herbert Hodges' *God beyond Knowledge* and Hugh Montefiori's *The Probability of God*. Hodges puts great stress on faith as decision:

> The well-informed believer treats God as one who addresses men and can be addressed by them, and lives on quasi-personal terms with God in all his affairs, while yet knowing all the time that it is with the Mystery that he is dealing . . .
> We do not know what God is like, but we know how to live with him: and our understanding of him, such as it is, is all in the living . . . The theist offers us not a proposition or a theory, but a life . . . To believe as against not believing is not to adopt an opinion, but to embrace a life . . .
> It is philosophy's business to show what existential choices are and why one cannot live without making them, it is not philosophy's business to make them . . . philosphy does not prove either view, but brings us to the point where the *man* decides.

Hugh Montefiore, an Anglican bishop, took a year off to investigate the intellectual grounds for belief in God in the light of the natural sciences today. His detailed findings make fascinating reading, for instance on the exact balance of constants, such as gravity or temperature, without which life

would be impossible on earth. Here we can only record a few
lines from his conclusion:

> The simplest explanation of what seem like extraordinary
> coincidences is that matter orders itself in a way that is
> optimal for life by the personal will of an omniscient and
> infinite God . . .

> Atheism remains always a possibility. But I would hold
> that *on the evidence atheism is wildly improbable* . . . In my
> judgment the convergence of all these factors makes it far,
> far more probable that God does exist than that he does
> not . . .

> We need to learn more about this God whose footsteps
> are to be seen in the wonders of his creation and in the
> experience of mankind. Our appetite for his revelation is
> whetted. Our thirst for his grace is awakened.

Step 7

Calls of Conscience

In the time of innocence I did not know that morality existed. I know it now.   Albert Camus

The plight of modern man: a sinner with no word for it.
                                                          Ernest Becker

Augustine started from the incompleteness of himself and searched for what would fill his emptiness. Aquinas started from the incompleteness of the world and asked where might lie the meaning that it lacked within itself. One journey involved painful self-struggle and the other rooted itself in a gentle yet powerful curiosity about everything. Our third road unites both temperaments in a new way, and can again be linked with another key figure in the history of the questioning about God. Several centuries after Aquinas, John Henry Newman spent a long life pondering the crisis of faith experienced in his world and coming up with his own angles of response.

His life spanned practically the entire nineteenth century, a time of unprecedented upheaval in England over the basics of religion. The turmoil was due in part to the extraordinary and rapid changes in society: for the first time in history a country had the majority of its people living in cities and large towns, and this meant the end of the sense of belonging, as had been characteristic of older rural communities. Side by side with this uprooting, new intellectual difficulties arose about faith. The dominant philosophy of empiricism found it impossible to acknowledge a God whom one could not prove in experimental fashion. Historical research began to accumulate doubts about the reliability of the scriptures. Many found their religious beliefs threatened by the evolution theories announced by Darwin. Although aware of all these issues, Newman's questions and answers lay deeper. From reflecting on the needs of his world and even more from probing his own personal experience, he proposed a new springboard for the credibility of faith. In his own words, 'self knowledge is at the root of all real religious knowledge'. In place of Augustine's emphasis on the hungers of the heart or the Aquinas focus on the questions of the mind, Newman was to put the experience of conscience and its struggles.

Newman often looked back at an experience he had as a teenager, which one can now see as a key to his whole thought. Although the details are not clear, it seems that he had some crisis at about fifteen which awoke him from a time of self-drifting into a dramatic sense of his own conscience. He experienced with painful urgency the conflict of right and wrong within himself, but through that experience he moved from what he would later call a 'notional' level of religion to a 'real assent' to the presence of God within him. In short, it was through the gateway of his own conscience that Newman first experienced faith as coming personally alive, and it is through this gateway that his many writings invite people to reconsider their often shaken and shaky faith.

Start from within yourself, he seems to insist; the real argument lies within you. Do you believe in your own self? If so, penetrate to the core of your selfhood by discovering the drama of your own conscience. That is the great interior guide to God – because it is in fact the voice of God. The main obstacles to faith are the 'aggressive intellect' which thinks it is the only way to truth, and even more so the 'proud self-sufficient spirit', the attitude of those who insist that they are the measure of all meaning and so cannot hear any voice higher than themselves. To experience your own conscience is a humbling business, which can rescue you from prisons of Rationalism (where reason alone is king) or Liberalism (which is soft on self and hazy about God). The truth of God cannot be demonstrated to the rationalist. Neither can the powerful calls of conscience be admitted by the liberal. But if you enter into the basic human experience of conscience, that brings about a different level of listening to reality – one that is rooted in reverence and can lead towards a sense of God. Newman's whole approach is to draw attention to a level of awareness that he believes to be present in everyone. It is a 'religious feeling' provoked by the experience of conscience. In his words, 'we believe because we love'. If some sense of reverence is not present, I am in danger of being caught in a cul-de-sac, expecting some infallible but impossible proof.

If Newman's foundation stone is the experience of conscience, his way forward towards faith is not merely intuitive or non-rational. Indeed few people have summarized his argument better than Thomas Hardy, who wrote in his diary after reading the *Apologia pro Vita Sua:* 'His logic [is] really human, being based not on syllogisms but on converging probabilities.' The atheist in Hardy remained unconvinced but what he admired as a really human logic was Newman's stress on disposition. If the basic attitude is cold and critical, there is no hope of progress toward faith. Unless a deep experience of conscience gives birth to a disposition of reverence, the tone will be wrong from the outset. With an attitude of awe, it is possible to find the right vein of reasoning which might open a road to God. Faith, for Newman, is never a deduction or conclusion but always 'a message, or a history, or a vision'. This more personal knowledge which is faith is 'created by probabilities', by converging paths which bring one to moral certitude but not to verifiable truth.

Start with self-reflection on the experience of conscience. Continue to ponder with reverence the probability of God. Such roads may lead to a 'real assent', a personal surrender well beyond the bounds of a merely intellectual truth.

This is the core of Newman's approach to faith. It is one that can be developed in different ways to meet the needs of today's culture. If I listen to the searchings of the younger generation now, I find that the experience of 'conscience' has changed in tone. It is not so much a private struggle between good and evil within the self – which is what Newman had most in mind – but rather a struggle of how to live in order to make a difference to this divided planet. Contemporary awareness fashions a wider world-conscience. People look beyond themselves at the hunger and woundedness of the Third World, or at the unjust distribution of opportunities within the First World, or at the struggle for peace and the threat of nuclear war, and from that exposure a new conscience awakens – less individualist, called to respond to realities bigger than the self. In one way it is an ancient story – as ancient as Moses being changed by hearing the cry of his own people in their oppression. At the core of the story is a cry arousing the heart from complacency into generosity. What am I going to do now that I have heard the cry of need? That is the painful question of today's conscience. Short-lived generosity is easy. How is the whole of life to be lived in ways that matter for others? That is the more frightening question – tougher, long-term, costly to self. To face that question is to encounter a twofold struggle of good and evil: within the value systems of the world and within the battle-zone of each self. To stay faithful to that experience of struggle is hard. It means encountering demons in various forms. There is the demon of despair born from the sheer enormity of the world's pain. There is the demon of guilt born from the constant failure of the self to live one's own hopes. At these points of impotence the need for some 'salvation' is experienced. And in this way God can come into view on the road of conscience – to some people as a voice of judgement and call, to others as the source of a desire to live a more generous life, and to others again as the saviour needed if I am to keep going along any road of steady loving.

One may close this part with a parable drawn from my own experience in India. I walked the streets of Calcutta one warm summer night. I stepped over a child who might have been asleep on the pavement, or he might have been sick, even dying. I came to eat my own meal but found I could not. The thought of the child came back again and again. So I put some of my own food in a bag and went in search of the child, who was still there, on the side of the street. I shook him gently till he awoke. He seemed frightened by this stranger in the night but he downed the food fast. Since we had no other language in common, I patted him on the head and left again. Back in my relatively comfortable room I tried to pray. I asked God why these things were allowed. Why did he not do something about so much pain? Was he all that all-mighty after all? I questioned in my anger and my fear and my guilt. Until at last, it was as if I heard the answer of God, from the quiet of my own conscience: 'But I am doing something – I made you'. (I had met this in one of Anthony de Mello's stories but now it was suddenly and powerfully my own.) Next morning I rose especially early to find the child again, determined to see what more could be done. He was no longer at the spot on the pavement, and the street was deserted – except for a child on the far side in the distance. He was rummaging in a rubbish bin but hurried round a corner when he seemed to notice me. Was he 'my child'? I will never know. I know only that his memory haunts me and it is through the image of him on that street that I hear those 'words of God': 'I am doing something about it – I made you.'

SCAFFOLDING FOR REFLECTION

> *In a world of fugitives*
> *The person taking the opposite direction*
> *Will appear to run away.*
>   T. S. Eliot

The object here will be to elicit a sense of life as call. Again and again I have heard something like this expressed by young people: 'I am here for something worthwhile, if only I could find it. I want to live a generous life, but how?' That crisis of frustrated commitment is one face of the crisis of faith in our time.

What is presented for reflection here will be philosophical and then meditative. First, an eloquent passage from Bernard Lonergan on the discovery of purpose in one's life:

> What, then, is commitment? Negatively, one might perhaps say that it is absent in the man or woman that just drifts through life, content to do what everyone else is doing, to say what everyone else is saying, to think what everyone else is thinking, where the 'everyone else' in question is just drifting too. Out of that company of drifters one steps when one faces the problem of personal existence; that is, when one finds out for oneself that one has to decide for oneself what one is to do with oneself, with one's life, with one's five talents or two or lonely one. Commonly such a

discovery, such a decision, such a programme of self-actualization becomes effective and irrecovable when one falls in love.

At one point in his *Spiritual Exercises* Ignatius Loyola proposes a parable to arouse enthusiasm – in order to prepare a person to hear the call of Christ. He imagines someone being invited by a king to join his companionship for a great and generous adventure. Will not recipients of this offer be overjoyed because the king has chosen to ask them? And so on. Leaving aside the sixteenth-century assumptions, can we find something similar for today?

Try this fantasy, giving it some quiet and time. Imagine yourself being told that you have only two years to live but that you will be able to retain your general health until the end. Then imagine yourself visiting some places of suffering that you know personally or at least by reputation: a hospice for the dying, a psychiatric hospital, a home for handicapped, a shelter for the homeless . . . Imagine that you greatly admire the dedication of the person in charge and that, much to your surprise, he or she says to you, 'If only you were free to be here with us – you are just the kind of person we need.' How would you respond to such a call?

To enter into that story, letting its initial implausibility fade, could be one way of unlocking one's generosity. In Newman's terms it would be an experience of conscience at its deepest. In Lonergan's sense it would be a way of emerging from drifting into commitment through the awakening of love.

Step 8

The Experience of Spirit

> *Was the pilgrimage*
> *I made to come to my own*
> *self, to learn that in times*
> *like these and for one like me*
> *God will never be plain and*
> *out there, but dark rather and*
> *inexplicable, as though he were in here?*
>   R. S. Thomas

There are times when one of those three roads convinces me and when faith seems obvious. At other times all I can sense is a more tentative pointing of the evidence in the direction of God. But there are moments when none of those ways seems to hold water, when a sceptical spirit reigns within me and the honest thing might be to declare myself an atheist once and for all. Or at least an agnostic. That point has never come and I don't believe it ever will. Why? Because of a fourth road that is both deep and mysterious, and hence difficult to put into words. Towards the end of his life Karl Rahner was questioned by an interviewer as to why he believed in God in spite of so many intellectual difficulties over faith today. The interviewer persisted in this line of inquiry to a degree that annoyed the famous theologian, who replied: 'Listen, I don't believe in God because I have worked everything out to the satisfaction of my mind. I continue to believe in God because I pray every day.' Within that frighteningly simple answer lies the clue to our fourth road: its evidence lies in the hard-to-fathom realm of religious experience.

When faith seems in deep trouble for me on an intellectual level, or because of the sheer unreality of it all in today's world, or in terms of the exasperating warts of church-life, the rock that I fall back on lies within my own personal prayer experience. There have been moments of power, which I can neither deny nor explain, but which remain anchors of my faith. There have been times when unexpectedly the veil seemed to lift and I knew some overwhelming sense of God. Down through the years these moments have been there, sometimes situated in the ordinary of life, sometimes in times of special retreat. Every year now for nearly twenty-five years, I have enjoyed a week of quiet and withdrawal, and every year that time has been marked by some 'proof' of God – in the sense that I encountered some experience of joy that was incomprehensible to me except as a sign of God's presence. The sadness of life is that I have not lived faithful to those moments, but without them I might have been even more astray. I recall them now with two purposes: to acknowledge them as the ultimate support of my faith and to hope that my experience can trigger off a recognition of such moments by others. In spite of the buffeting that faith takes within me, and in spite of the many times when I think to myself that I might as well be an atheist, those brushes with grace have been my salvation. It is not that I think about them often. It is rather that it would be a contradiction for me to turn away from a faith that has been nourished by such experiences. I am convinced that most people have similar experiences of the spirit, which can also serve them as pointers to faith.

As a patron figure for this fourth road, I think of that great woman of the spirit, Teresa of Avila. Her story is a fascinating one, with its years of unsteadiness before she finally reached surrender. For a long time she seems to have been a most human mixture of huge ideals and predictable mediocrity. There is the famous episode, when she was only seven, of setting forth with her young brother to seek martyrdom at the hands of the Moors, only to run into the reality principle of an uncle who happened to be on the road. Then she seems to have fallen into ways of vanity and frivolity as a beautiful young girl – or so she says of herself in her autobiography. But at the age of twenty she entered the local Carmelite convent and quickly discovered her capacity for a 'prayer of quiet and even of union'. With another swing of the pendulum she stopped praying and spent her time in long conversations

with visitors to the convent; even though she might be coun-
selling them towards contemplative levels of prayer, for some
years she herself avoided prayer. She moved from 'pastime
to pastime' but kept the outward appearance of a spiritual
life. Inside her all was evasion and false fear of God. 'I was
following the world', she said later, 'unable to shut myself
within myself.' This time of drifting lasted only a few years
and from about her mid-twenties Teresa began again to have
some kind of spiritual life, except that it was dominated by
dryness and conflict. This 'war' went on for twenty 'weary'
years, marked by small consolation and little hope: it was
shadowed by ill-health and even more by a sense of failure,
an inability to give herself to God without reserve.

It seemed as if the dreams of childhood and the graces of
her early years in Carmel were doomed to unfulfilment, when
suddenly, in her early forties, everything changed within.
Praying one day before a new painting of the passion, Teresa
not only found the freedom to let go of her dividedness of
heart but to enter into a new level of rapture as a 'servant of
love'. From then on, her remaining twenty-five years were
marked by extraordinary experiences of grace and equally
extraordinary energy as a leader and reformer of religious life.
In both roles she became celebrated throughout Spain, as a
mystic and as a powerful force for change. She wrote enor-
mously and with attractive freshness about the contemplative
life. Her autobiography offers one of the most down-to-earth
expressions of the mystical life ever written:

> Sometimes even when reading, I would unexpectedly
> experience a consciousness of the presence of God, of such
> a kind I could never doubt that He was within me or that
> I was completely engulfed in Him . . . The soul seems to
> be completely outside itself. The will loves. The memory,
> I think, is almost lost; while the understanding does not
> work to reason, it is amazed at the extent of all it can
> understand.

An atheist of aggressive disposition could dismiss such
statements as self-delusion. But there are unbelievers with a
more open and reverent attitude to the mysteries of human
experience and they can find in Teresa of Avila one of the
great witnesses to the possibility of an adventure of the spirit.

There can be no mistaking the authenticity of the woman and her words:

> There came to me a transport so sudden that it almost carried me away. I could make no mistake about it, so clear it was. This was the first time that the Lord granted me the grace of any rapture. I heard these words, 'I will have thee converse now, not with men but with angels'. This simply amazed me, for my soul was greatly moved and the words were spoken to me in the depths of the spirit . . . Since that day I have had courage to give up everything for the sake of God, who in that moment was pleased to make His servant into another person.

Such witnesses as Teresa force on us lesser mortals a realization of those 'depths of the spirit'. Not only does she witness to her own experience but she can evoke neglected spiritual glimpses of each person, bringing them out into fuller awareness. It may be no accident that Teresa was a woman, because what she records is that essentially feminine receptivity whether in women or men.

What then is the evidence of our fourth road? People claim that they have had experiences that come from God: they offer no proof except their own overwhelming sense of his presence and perhaps the fruits of that experience in a life of freedom and love. There can be little question of verifying this evidence in any usual sense. But since it often forms the bedrock of people's quiet confidence that God exists and that they have known him, it must at least be listed as one of the great pointers towards faith in God.

SCAFFOLDING FOR REFLECTION

If God is God, he is likely to be the most common of human experiences: people keep bumping into Him all the time, but that is not what they call Him. John V. Taylor

Our singling out of Teresa of Avila could be dangerous if it equated religious experience with the extraordinary moments of extraordinary people. Such peak experiences may be important as personal turning points, but if there is a God, he must be encountered most in the ordinary. Otherwise he becomes a God of Rarified Reality Only, or someone who triggers off the universe and then is seldom seen, like an absentee landlord.

The Teresa story is only a reminder of our potential richness. What is manifest in the drama of her life is a process that happens hiddenly in many everyday ways, and in people who may make little explicit reference to God. This emphasis on religious experience in the ordinary has been strong in recent thinking, as can be seen in different ways in three of the most distinguished of modern theologians.

We draw again on Bernard Lonergan who offers an enticingly succinct set of 'precepts' for fulfilling the 'demands of the human spirit': 'Be attentive, be intelligent, be reasonable, be responsible, be in love'. In other words there are five levels of human growth (or decline). After attending to the range of one's experience and seeking insights that gather it together, after arriving at truth and reaching commitments, on a fifth level comes the 'complete self-transcendence' of a 'deep-set joy' through being-in-love with God. But this more contemplative possibility is not to be separated from the overall 'struggle of authenticity' that is the story of each life on all levels.

Hans Urs von Balthasar can also be called to give evidence on this point. As a great defender of a contemplative approach to faith, he stresses that the experience of God involves a perceiving of radiant beauty and a surrender to enrapturing love. Some sentences of his can serve to gather up at least three of the traditions of quest which we have been exploring here: 'In an Augustinian and Thomistic sense, the creature experiences its innermost fulfilment and the quieting of its unrest when, in a transcending manner, it abandons itself to the gravitational pull of its love for God.' But he sees these two approaches – the more existential longing of Augustine for what is *good* and the more theoretical quest of Aquinas for what is *true* – as requiring also an experience of God as *beautiful*. The beautiful demands 'that we renounce our attempts to control and manipulate it, in order truly to be able to be happy enjoying it'. But von Balthasar is at pains to broaden this stress on 'aesthetic' experience of faith and to rescue it from being reduced to special moments. He sees it as entailing a transformation of one's whole way of life through a gradual 'attunement to God'.

Karl Rahner would go further in insisting that the God-experience is not to be identified with mystical moments. In his way of thinking each person has an inescapable, even if unacknowledged, experience of God; in the depths of each life, one is either saying 'yes' or 'no' to love and thus to God. If the option and general direction of one's existence is towards 'selfless surrender', this must show itself as an experience of God in actual life. For Rahner the essential sign of this experience lies in loving others 'without reward or advantage', God's Spirit being at work whenever 'a person really goes beyond himself'. In his own challengingly lucid words, 'the personal history of the experience of the self is the personal history of the experience of God'.

A CONVERGENCE OF QUESTS

Inability to explain is no ground for disbelief. Not as long as the sense of God persists. Saul Bellow

We have received this gift from the hands of SOMEONE.
Alexander Solzhenitsyn

We have listened to four witnesses who, in fascinatingly different ways, searched for God. What they share is that their quest stories started from some deep hunger within themselves. Those four layers are in each of us – the emotional self, the intellectual self, the spiritual self and the person of moral conscience. Our quartet of celebrated searchers can find many echoes in today's world. I think of a modern 'Augustine' for whom sex-without-strings ultimately proved stifling; only after a long time and with painful honesty did he recognize this, and this recognition put him in touch with even deeper hungers – for love and for God. I know an 'Aquinas', highly qualified in science and alienated from traditional religion. Behind his professionalism a constant quest went on for some satisfying approach to faith, and his breakthrough came through a sentence of Rudolf Steiner's: 'No one suggests that light is simply something that goes on in the eye.' I can think of a 'Newman', a young woman who tried many lifestyles and seemed unable to find anything to meet her hopes, until eventually she opted for 'downward mobility', devoting herself to the handicapped. I have met many a secret 'Teresa', people with a sense of depth within them, who often remain unfulfilled because they can find no steady expression for the interior richness that is theirs.

Along all four roads, Mozart can be murdered (a phrase from Antoine de Saint-Exupéry). Gifts that might bear fruit fall into disuse. Hungers can lie neglected that if followed might lead towards faith. Thus the Augustine and the Aquinas, the Newman and the Teresa in us can either be killed or given space to expand and live. Those four dimensions are crucial for any definition of humanity, because each person is an amalgam of feeling and thought, of freedom and self-transcendence. When such central strands of the self point together in one direction, their convergence is surely significant.

As admitted earlier, I shy away from talking of 'proof' in this matter of God. But the coming together of these pointers has been a powerful source of conviction for me. My favourite image for it is of the convergence of four spotlights on a stage. One light casts shadows but gradually the converging of four lights, from different angles, creates a pool of light without shadows. Similarly there can be much shadow in the search for God. I can see flaws in any single argument. I can doubt the conclusiveness of the evidence of the heart alone, or mind alone, or conscience alone, or spirit alone. But the accumulating evidence of the four seems so much more convincing – like many lights cancelling the shadows. These roads then are human pointers that bring me, not to faith, but to the possibility of faith. Christian faith does not depend on these ways of thinking out the issue of God's existence. These converging roads can help make sense of faith and defend it from the scepticism of everyday. But, as we shall see, faith itself is born from love, not from these pointers that merely help towards credibility and towards the threshold of faith.

For me the Christian answer offers:
– a vision that most satisfies the mind,
– a person that meets the hopes of the heart,

– a way of life that fulfils and challenges the conscience,
– and a sense of gift that overwhelms the spirit.
But to talk of the Christian answer is already to go beyond
the focus of this section. Our quest stories need to be
completed by love stories.

Part 3

Love Stories

Our wartime escape stories had three stages: getting ready, getting away, getting out of enemy territory. Although those stages are not exactly parallel to the three main divisions of this book, there are some similarities. Our escape stories dealt with readiness for freedom, through getting rid of false dispositions and obstacles. Then our quest stories showed how people get out of themselves and travel their different roads to faith. What we shall call love stories are like the long journey from prison through danger towards final freedom. Escaping war-prisoners often met with friends and foes on their road; it seems to have been impossible to make that journey without help. Who meets us on our road? Who is with us as we try to find freedom? These questions lead into the final two steps here: they point us towards the gospels as visions of life. And at the centre of that gospel vision is the extraordinary claim that we are joined by God in the freedom-journey of our humanity.

We arrive then at a new threshold. We have tried to evoke four struggles of freedom and then four avenues towards religious meaning. All eight 'steps' so far have a shared starting-point: they come from the blockages and yearnings of our humanity and in this sense they all begin 'from below'. We turn now to the strange possibility of God's revelation, which is by definition 'from above' or beyond us. To cross this threshold means a change of wavelength, because if God has spoken to us, all our striving and questing become secondary. They remain important as part of our honest journeying, but they are secondary to the overwhelming possibility that God draws near to us and addresses us. If this is true, we stop being the centre of our world, and the main plot of existence is not about our searching for him but about his searching for us. Buddhism and Hinduism, for instance, are rich traditions embodying this long quest for spiritual wisdom. But Christianity is something else because at its core is a quite different quest: the coming of God into humanity to seek us out. That search takes the form of a love story.

Step 9

Christ Encounter

A religion which is perfectly at home in the world has no counsel for it which the world could not gain by an easier method.

Reinhold Niebuhr

It would be possible for atheist friends to share much of our journey to this point, with its double search – for freedom and meaning. Now we come to a fork in the road and our ways may part. All that has gone before brings us to this choice. We may have become more open to the possibility of faith (escape stories). The convergence of traditional wisdom may be impressive in pointing towards God (quest stories). But how can we encounter this possible God? Where is the evidence that he shows any interest in us?

The answer that we are to explore here comes from the love story of Jesus Christ. 'Who do you say that I am'? To his own question there can be no 'perhaps'. Either this man was the human face of God or else millions have based their lives on an illusion. My unbelieving friends might not accept that stark either-true-or-false. They might regard the historical figure of Jesus as a great religious leader, a spiritual genius, someone who embodies the hopes of humanity to live with love. They might see his story as a poem of visionary inspiration. They might reverence his life and death as they would that of Gandhi or Martin Luther King. But without crossing the threshold into faith they cannot reach what is central to the vision of Jesus in the gospels – a relationship with God as his Father and a conviction that he came from God to inaugurate a new way of living called the Kingdom.

THE THRESHOLD OF FAITH

> *If the scientific method monopolizes all ways of thinking, it can
> damage the certitude unique to faith, where knowledge is also love.
> Likewise the spirit of continual research tends to suspend judgement;
> in this way it risks remaining always at the threshold of faith.*
>
> Pope John Paul II

Much could be said about this different route to faith that is
'revelation'. Let us leave aside the valid questions about the
historical truth of the gospels and for the moment face the
concreteness of the Christian story. As one girl said to me,
only last December: 'I don't like Christmas, not because of
all the superficiality, but because it's too definite for me – a
baby that they say is God'. Her statement captured one of
the great blockages to Christianity in modern culture: Christ
is embarrassingly definite. This Jesus is scandalously real, not
some misty presence. Burdened with our sense of today's
complexities, we feel easier when we reverence from afar, or
more comfortable when we can stay tentative. The temptation
of our time is to rest content with the 'old interior itch'
(Walker Percy) and become stuck in perpetual searching. The
four quest stories were rich highways but they need not add
up to faith. That more complete 'yes' comes from, in some
way, 'hearing' the Word.

But the revelation of Christ has been a stumbling block in
different ways to different cultures. The earliest Christian
centuries did not dare represent the horror of the crucifixion.
In the nineteenth century the claims of revelation seemed
magical and mythical to a rationality proudly aware of its
achievements. In this century we seem to know so much that
we can decide with confidence about so little – hence our
frequent vagueness about concrete truth and concrete
commitments. It can seem more honest to remain in a threshold stance, wondering but waiting.

As opposed to that stance of hesitation, faith takes the risk
of crossing the threshold. What is this faith? And how is it
possible? To tackle those questions, we turn briefly to the
theologians and then to the gospels themselves.

Down through the centuries theology has pondered the

paradoxes of faith and tried to cast light on its strangeness. This long tradition seems agreed on some basics:
- that faith is a free response and yet a gift of God;
- that it involves assent of the mind and yet trust in a Person;
- that it is reasonable to believe and yet it is an encounter with Mystery;
- that faith remains obscure because of the unsteadiness of ourselves and of our understanding, and yet it reaches certainty because of the steadiness of God himself.

The first element in each pairing is the approach to faith 'from below' – or the human effort seen in our 'escape stories' and 'quest stories'. The second half in each looks to the way of revelation 'from above' – which is God's gift, to be explored now as 'love stories'.

An earlier section touched on the Aquinas definition of faith as 'an act of the intellect commanded by the' will'. Aquinas was marvellously blunt about how unusual faith is: it does not start from external data because in that sense there can be no data on God. Therefore it will be an 'incomplete knowledge', always fragile if judged by the criteria of common-sense knowing. Where other kinds of knowledge are acts of the intellect, building on the data of the senses, faith involves an element of choice ('commanded by the will'), and this is the key to its differentness.

But choice about what? I have sometimes enjoyed myself in seminars on faith by offering this Aquinas definition and then another definition from the modern theologian, Bernard Lonergan. He speaks of faith as 'a knowledge born of love' when 'God's love is flooding our hearts'. It was intriguing to find that people left cold by the language of Aquinas might murmur with delight at Lonergan's phrase. But the two thinkers are saying the same thing! The 'will' is where 'love' originates, and 'knowledge' is precisely 'an act of the intellect'. Both descriptions underline the specialness of faith as a way of knowing: it involves a choice to recognize love.

This is what some theologians mean by an 'epistemological break' or a 'crucifixion of the intellect' before one can arrive at faith. At one point in the gospels Jesus rejoices that faith is revealed to children while hidden from the clever (Luke 10:21). Or as Jon Sobrino puts it, faith challenges our usual

'frames of interpretation'. It is not verifiable in any normal
sense: it mocks the merely 'clever' mind.

THE GOSPEL IN THE PRESENT TENSE

*Instead of looking at Jesus to learn what God is like and how we
go to him, we project on to Jesus our ideas of God, and so lose sight
of him . . . Apart from Jesus we know nothing of God.*

Ruth Burrows

It is time to 'come and see' the New Testament answer to
our struggles and searchings, the answer embodied in Jesus
Christ. But how are we to read these strange documents, the
Scriptures? Many fall into a merely factual approach to the
gospels, as events recorded from Palestine two thousand years
ago. They are that in their own way, but also much more.
They are love stories that need to be rescued from being
merely records of the past in order to be experienced as stories
of power in the present.

A lot of my life has been given to studying texts, either
as a teacher of literature or as trying to base my religious
commitment on the gospels. Over the years I have come to
realize that a crucial difference exists between these two kinds
of writing. There can be a deep truth in literature, but ultimately it is imaginary. There can be a great wisdom in
history, but ultimately it is past. The claim of the gospels is
quite different. The truth of these stories is neither imaginary
nor past. They took place at a certain time in history, but
their real truth is in the present. The gospel stories are forever
being rewritten in the present – by their first author, the Holy
Spirit.

Without a present-tense encounter with the Jesus of the
gospels Christian faith will be either stunted or else impossible. Faith in its full sense means more than arriving at the
conclusion 'yes there is a God'. That might be a reasonable
belief 'from below', but faith involves a love-gift 'from above'.
Our steps so far could help a person towards theism – but
Christian faith is something else. It leaves behind *our* escape
and quest stories in order to hear *God's* love stories; faith
happens when the stories meet.

THE MEETING OF THE STORIES

God made man because he loves stories. Elie Wiesel

In the gospels the meeting of human need and Christ's compassion gives rise to a particular pattern of plot. In John's gospel, for instance, the first and last 'signs' of Jesus show a striking similarity in one respect. The first episode is the wedding at Cana and the last is the risen Christ on the shore of Lake Tiberias. Both events move from emptiness to fullness: from having no wine to having the best wine, and from having caught nothing all night to a net so full of fish that at first they could not haul it in.

Many of the encounters of Jesus with individuals offer variations on that movement from lack into lavishness. Towards the beginning of John's gospel there is a fascinating little drama of a sceptic being gradually set free for faith. It starts with Philip who, the previous day, had been 'found' by Jesus and invited to 'follow' him. Now he wants to share his excitement but his friend Nathaniel seems to pour cold water on his enthusiasm. It is like the moment in escape stories where one prisoner wakes up to the fact that it is possible to escape, only to find his fellow prisoners dubious about his bright idea. Nathaniel seems incapable of hope, or unable to imagine new possibilities for himself. I have heard his question – 'Can anything good come out of Nazareth?' – echoed in the scepticism of other Nathaniels of today. I recall one young man whose initial moment of doubt came at the first Easter Vigil ceremony he attended as an ordinary member of the congregation. Previously he had always been at the centre, as an altar boy, but now he was on the margins and unconvinced by the words and gestures. The priests themselves did not seem to believe. The ritual did not communicate resurrection. He sensed a dishonesty in the event. That instant of non-belonging led to a long journey of questioning and questing. His Nathaniel note showed itself in a wariness of official religion, in a caution lest he be taken in too easily again. It was as if he were saying, 'Can anything good come of the Catholicism I once knew?'

Others live that Nathaniel question in different ways: somewhere a hurt happened and self-doubt was born. Yeats in his

great poem 'Among School Children' evokes memories of
childhood pain:

> a harsh reproof, or trivial event
> That changed some childish day to tragedy.

I think of one girl humiliated before her classmates about the
age of twelve, when due to nervousness she could not answer
a question; the teacher made her stand on a chair and keep
her mouth wide open for five minutes – as a sign of her being
an 'empty fool'. Something snapped within her after that
ordeal. Childhood was never the same again and, as she put
it, she retreated behind her face 'in silence and fear'.

Small events can cast long shadows. In listening to people's
stories, I have been amazed at how often that change-to-
tragedy happened through one incident of punishment or
mockery. Thus another Nathaniel is born, for whom 'can
anything good come out of Nazareth?' in fact means 'can
anything good come out of Nathaniel?' When self-worth is
wounded, a whole language of faith – human and religious –
may stutter or fall silent. This is not to explain all religious
difficulties away as due to some psychological hurt, but
unreadiness for revelation can have roots in this area of a
person's life. I remember asking a young agnostic once
whether he had ever been in love. He answered that he had
felt locked up in himself for years and worried if he could
ever love or be loved. His facing of this previously unacknowledged self-doubt was his first step on a Nathaniel road of
'coming' and 'seeing'.

FROM SCEPTICISM TO SEEING

*There were many who saw the evidence, materially, but did not
believe – did not see with the eyes the Spirit gives.*   John Coventry

What is called 'coming' in this gospel episode is something I
have seen happen for many people: they begin by voicing
hesitations over faith, only to find themselves expressing shy
hopes for something deeper that might make sense of their
experience. Philip invited Nathaniel to try what he himself
had experienced: come and see. And in John's gospel those

simple monosyllables do not mean any ordinary 'walk down the road and have a look'. Rather they invite Nathaniel to 'come' with his whole self and to 'see' with the eyes of the heart. This happens when people get in touch with their true selves (which, as we saw, means escaping from the false self). 'Jesus saw Nathaniel coming to him'; this is deeper than a journey of the feet. Although still dubious, he has begun to awaken to hope, to move towards a point of listening and transformation.

The next moment of this story is the recognition of the smothered goodness in Nathaniel. Jesus greets him as a worthy Israelite, incapable of being dishonest – which must at first sound strange to the cynic in him. It is as if this praise tries to penetrate through that mask to the real Nathaniel. But initially this welcome is met with another sceptical question: 'How do you know me?' I hear this question spoken in a tone of mixed suspicion and surprise. There is suspicion because he is not used to strangers who walk into his life with personal and positive responses. There is surprise because this stranger is expressing acceptance and appreciation of him. The Nathaniels I have known feel more comfortable keeping people at a certain distance. Trespassers will be prosecuted – because to be known might risk rejection.

Nathaniel's moment of faith in the Messiah needs a first moment of restored faith in himself. This comes about through one of the most inexplicable sayings in the whole gospel: 'I saw you under the fig tree'. Many guesses have been made about its meaning, but of one thing I am sure: it must have been a happy secret, a joyful mystery of Nathaniel's life. If not, it would never have evoked the response of 'seeing' in faith that he now blurts out: 'You are the Son of God'. There is always good news behind the bad news, always hidden treasure in the field; once that true self is free, the door is open to recognizing a Christ of love. But at this point Jesus seems to tease him, even to laugh at the leap he had just taken: 'You say *that* because I said I saw you under the fig tree! You will see greater things.' Starting from the first contact by Philip, Nathaniel has now come into transforming contact with God embodied in Jesus – and that is *the* foundation of Christian faith.

Here then is a headline story for this ninth step towards

faith, and one that finds echoes in our culture of today. Nathaniels abound, and their first need on the road to faith is contact with a Philip, a believer who invites. Perhaps even a book like this can take the place of Philip. That first contact can awaken a willingness in the doubter to trust their own stories and yet allow a meeting with the Jesus story. If the unbeliever tries to 'come and see' in this way, what might he or she find in the gospels? Not a religion of narrowness or a God of negativity but a welcoming 'yes' of recognition. When fig trees are glimpsed, the smothered self is set free. The 'yes' of Christ's understanding is echoed shyly by the 'yes' of dawning faith. Because that is what faith is – a yes to a yes, a human yes of recognition spoken to a divine yes of love: faith is the vision arising from being loved.

THE GOSPEL AS FULFILMENT

Jesus is the final call of God, and after him no others follow.

Karl Rahner

After the constant refrain of the Old Testament that God will fulfil the heart's desires, the New Testament presents Christ as meeting in his own self the hungers of humanity for freedom, for meaning, and ultimately for love. So before concluding this ninth step, I want to list ways in which the gospel both completes and transforms what was at the core of each previous 'step'. It is as if the Christ of revelation says: 'I am the goal of all your journeys so far – listen and you will hear.'

And so we review our eight steps, in order to notice a marvellous correspondence between our struggling and the promises of Jesus Christ.

(1) The battle of the false and the true self now becomes interpersonal – the possibility of a saviour who comes to forgive our sins. In the Greek of the New Testament the word for sin is *hamartia*, which is literally a missing of the mark, as in archery. Hence sin means falling below the target of a full and loving freedom in our humanity; and forgiveness means

that a liberator is at hand, someone who understands, heals and sets free from the imprisonment of the false self.

(2)   Similarly the struggle of a true and false society is given flesh in such words as 'nobody can serve two masters' (Matt. 6:24). But again the social gospel has a personal centre: in Jesus we see the beginning of God's revolution against the selfish mess of our history. In him we have the Beatitudes not only spoken but lived. His resistance-movement, called 'the Kingdom', has not only a founder but a leader who promises to remain with his struggling friends.

(3)   The gospel version of the 'wrong question' is captured in the words 'unless you become as a little child you cannot enter the kingdom' (Luke 18:17). A similar insistence is found in St Paul, for whom 'the philosophy of our age' is not only incapable of 'understanding the gifts of God' but amounts to 'foolishness' in matters of the spirit (1 Cor. 2:6,12; 3:19). In the New Testament, then, faith requires a prior disposition of reverence and trust, and if that attitude is missing, love cannot be discerned. In the words of the Magnificat, 'the hungry he has filled with good things, the rich sent empty away' (Luke 1:53).

(4)   All the pitfalls of human thinking about God are transformed and even banished by the central claim of the incarnation. To be a Christian means someone who discovers God through Christ. As St Paul simply says, 'He is the image of the unseen God' (Col. 1:15). Or in Pascal's view it is impossible to come to true faith in God without a sense of the person of Jesus Christ.

(5)   Turning from our four escape struggles to our four quests, the Jesus of the Scriptures (particularly John's gospel) is seen as *the* answer to the hungers of humanity. We are invited to 'come' with our restlessness and our burdens, to discover that all can become 'gentle' and 'easy' (Matt. 11:28–30). 'I myself am the bread of life. No one who comes to me shall ever be hungry, no one who believes in me shall ever thirst' (John 6:35). All of Augustine's desires remained

unfocused and astray until they eventually found such undreamed-of satisfaction in the presence of Christ.

(6) Likewise with the question of truth, John's gospel can see this only in radically personal terms. Jesus himself is the one 'who has told you the truth which I have heard from God' (John 8:40). In his own self he is 'the way and the truth and the life' (John 14:6). It is living in discipleship with him that allows one to 'know the truth', that truth which 'will set you free' (John 8:32). This view of truth begins and ends with the person of Jesus and so is at a complete remove from the 'fact-worship', as Herbert Marcuse has termed it, of modern culture.

(7) Our seventh step concerned fidelity to the calls of conscience. Jesus in the gospels is seen as making fun of the religiosity of the 'Lord, Lord' variety if it is divorced from 'doing the will of my Father'. The entire twenty-fifth chapter of Matthew is devoted to three parables, all of which stress the necessity of accepting responsibility for this world. Don't expect others to have oil for your lamps; you have to make sure of it yourself. Don't bury your talent in the ground out of fear; use it. Don't expect to meet Christ in some obvious way; what you do to the least of people you do to him. One may remember the saying of Ignatius Loyola: pray as if everything depended on God but act as if everything depended on you.

(8) Our eighth step was the area of religious experience. This dimension of human searching 'from below' finds its New Testament complement in the gift of the Spirit 'from above'. From a multitude of possible texts I shall single out just a few. The climax of the teaching of Jesus on prayer stresses how the Father desires 'to give the Holy Spirit to those who ask him' (Luke 11:13). There are the Last Supper promises of Jesus to send the Paraclete, who 'will teach you everything' and 'guide you to all truth' (John 14:26; 16:13). The Letter to the Romans abounds in references to the Spirit: it is through the gift of the Spirit that 'the love of God is poured into our hearts': it is through the evidence of 'our spirit' united with 'the Spirit' that we know ourselves to

belong as children to God (Rom. 5:5; 8:16). In other words the role of the Spirit is crucial for faith. Moreover, there exists a meeting point between our questing spirit and the gift of the Holy Spirit, an experience that confirms our faith in the first love story – our being loved by God.

Much more could be added under each of those eight headings. But enough has been said to realize how a Christ-encounter can meet the deep hungers of our humanity. At this crucial stage in our imagined journey towards faith, all comes together into a powerful and personal convergence. Can our hope stories find fulfilment in the love story of Jesus Christ? For it is from the meeting of those stories that faith is born.

SCAFFOLDING FOR MEDITATION

That meeting will never happen from reading a book of this kind, or at least from reading it in a spirit of detached curiosity. I can introduce one person to another in the firm hope that they are made for one another, but so much will depend on their approach and the level of their meeting one another. So too with this ninth step toward faith. It needs a special openness before the encounter can get beyond surface chat. In the unbeliever there can be an allergy to 'Jesus talk' – because much of it has been merely pious or insulting to human complexity. Many 'believers' may also need to cross this threshold into a personal sense of Christ.

What is offered here consists of two scenes from the gospels, as material for meditation. Both are akin to the Nathaniel story in that they tell of the coming to faith of a wounded individual. If approached in a spirit of objective neutrality or suspicion, these stories will remain, at most, interesting. But with some stillness, hunger and if possible prayerfulness, these scenes can come powerfully to life.

A dramatic episode in this respect is the story of Bartimaeus in chapter 10 of Mark's gospel. Allow yourself to identify with this blind beggar on the roadside. In what sense do you not see? In what sense are you in need? A crowd passes. Jesus is said to be there. Suddenly Bartimaeus starts to shout out

hoping to attract the attention of this Jesus. But he only
annoys people, who tell him to keep quiet. Let yourself
become aware of the many voices, inside and outside, that
stifle your hopes for faith. But Bartimaeus shouts even more.
And an exciting message comes. Jesus has stopped for him.
'Rise up. Take heart. He is calling you.' Rich phrases evoking
new life, new courage, new possibilities of companionship.
Bartimaeus in his urgency jumps up and even already flings
away the sign of his shame – the beggar's cloak. And he
'comes' to Jesus (in the deep sense – as with Nathaniel), only
to hear the question 'What do you want me to do for you?'
To see again – with the eyes and also with the heart. 'Your
faith has made you well.' In Albert Nolan's comment, 'faith
releases within us a power that is beyond us'. Finally Bartimaeus is not only able to 'see' but able to follow 'on the way',
that is, to enter the Kingdom way of life with Jesus. His is a
story of struggle to escape from blindness into faith.

In John's gospel, chapter 4, we find the most extended
dialogue in all the gospels, and it is like the conversation of
humanity with God. It moves from resistance to the recognition that is faith. You can watch Jesus struggling, as it were,
to bring this difficult and wounded woman to the threshold of
new freedom. At the outset she refused him even a drink of
water, but by the end she has discovered the living water of
who-he-is, the promised saviour.

This text of the gospel could be read through in less than
two minutes, but to yield its riches would need a slower and
more contemplative approach. Then one will discover a Jesus
who, as Rosemary Haughton has put it, is 'furiously tender
to the damaged and the weak'. Notice also the various stages
within this journey of freedom. Notice how the conversation
takes place, ironically, on two levels: his level of offering living
water and her imprisonment in the familiar, reducing it to
'you have no bucket'. Her way to faith is blocked by this
mentality, and in a host of other ways: her argumentativeness
over the past (Jacob's well); her half-evasion of the pains of
her own personal life (five broken relationships); her surface
questioning over religion (should we have worship in the
temple or on the mountain?); and her final ploy is to postpone
any surrender into some vague future (when the Messiah will
come).

Each of these resistances is present in everyone. Coming through them is a major step towards faith. But faith becomes possible in this scene when the moment is ripe for Jesus to reveal himself and to bring the conversation into the present tense: I who am speaking to you, I am he. Suddenly all changes. With marvellous symbolism she puts down her water jar and carries the news to the city. The Christ plot has been played again – from emptiness to fullness, and a fullness that then overflows.

Step 10

Down and Out

Knowledge of God without knowing our own poverty makes for pride. Knowledge of our own poverty without knowing God makes for despair. Knowledge of Jesus Christ lets us be present both to God and to our poverty. Blaise Pascal

Everything that was said of Jesus in Step Nine could be too soft, if it stopped there. The full love story has different tones within it. Not only is there a movement from emptiness to fullness, but another movement from trusting in Jesus to being shaken by him. Many of his initial encounters with people brought them consolation; only later on were they confronted with the price of living his kind of love. It is all too easy to present an attractive half-Jesus – a god of mere consolation (like those false images we pondered earlier). But that 'god' rightly alienates the more alert searchers of today. A friend of mine, who considers herself religious in her own way, has often expressed to me her criticism of the glibness of church religion and the cheapness of some Christian 'good news'. This tenth step is dedicated to her.

Now the tables are turned. So far we have been doing the questioning, but here we find ourselves radically questioned by the gospel.

THREE SECRETS

We instinctively refuse to try the way that leads through darkness.
C. G. Jung

The Christian love story has a double plot that could be entitled 'down and out': the first story is about love coming down and the second about love going out. It could be visualized as an upside-down capital 'T', and it is what is at the heart of John's letter in the New Testament. Having announced with transparent clarity that 'God is love', he goes on to two further surprises. First comes his Copernican revolution: the starting point for Christian faith is *not* our love for God but God's love for us'. Familiarity can dim the explosiveness of that negative and positive. Religion is commonly thought of as something-I-have-to-do, but the first secret is the firstness of God's loving.

If it were up to me, how would I finish the sentence: 'Since God has loved us so much, we too should . . . ?' Love him in return? No! John channels the flow of love in another way: 'We too should love one another' (1 John 4:10–11). Here lies the second secret: our love for God is expressed indirectly. Most of the time we cannot love him directly, consciously; but we can always try to live with love for the people and the planet he has given us.

So far so good. But something darker has to be faced as well, which I will call down-and-out-ness: to explain this another personal memory may help. I remember some days of generous joy when I was first working in Mother Teresa's home for the dying in Calcutta. There was nothing I could not do. I was walking on air from the happiness of being there at all. Then one day when I was dabbing lotion on an old man's back (because he had scabies), the man in the next bed started to shout out for tea. 'Chai, chai'. I told him I would get it for him in a few minutes. But then as I continued to tend the other man's sores, the thirsty patient took to poking me in the back with his finger as he continued to call for 'chai'. It was too much. I turned on him and told him in no uncertain tone that he could wait till I had finished. The dream evaporated; the saint was no more. I came down with a thud into my usual far-from-patient self. I had not changed very much after all. Why do I remain unsteady in loving? Christ's answer is that I find it hard to let go of my own self.

In that Calcutta moment I was forced to recognize my own poverty. Just when I seemed to be living the full flow of the down-love and the out-love. I ran into the humiliation of my down-and-out-ness. In the pain of this self-poverty lies a third secret: 'It is when I am weak that I am strong' (2 Cor.

12:10). As Edward Schillebeeckx has put it, 'There is a human impotence which God alone can relieve.' That very impotence can prove to be a pulley: what weighs down can also raise up.

This is one of the hardest paradoxes on any road towards faith. It asks me to own with humbling honesty the darkest areas of self-failure. It asks me to acknowledge my bankruptcy of love. If the Christ plot is to lead me from emptiness to fullness, it demands an admission of that basic emptiness. And this is where 'human kind', in T. S. Eliot's words, 'cannot bear very much reality'.

THE GOSPEL AS CONLFICT

Either one secures for oneself one's place in the 'system', or one puts oneself in one's poverty and defencelessness at the source point from which everything springs, without reason or system, from the freedom of love.   Hans Urs von Balthasar

Arriving at faith can depend on the outcome of this essential conflict between pride and poverty. Pride here is quite different from vanity. Pride means a closed system with no needs. Vanity, as shown in attention-seeking is rooted rather in insecurity. Pride can be cultural as well as personal because our world avoids powerlessness in all its forms. Poverty, as used here, is obviously not economic. Like pride it is a radical disposition; it means a self-knowing that admits the humbling truth but without grovelling. It is a spiritual attitude which becomes a source of hunger and of thankful trust, as in the Magnificat: 'The hungry he has filled with good things, the rich sent empty away' (Luke 1:53).

It is right here – in the battle-zone of pride and poverty – that the Jesus of the gospels fights for our full freedom and remains always dissatisfied with half-freedom. Initially he invites people to healing, acceptance, trust; but sooner or later comes the tougher truth, the challenge to any easy complacencies. There is the Jesus of 'Come to me, all you who labour and are overburdened, and I will give you rest' (Matt. 11:28). There is also the Jesus of 'unless a wheat grain falls on the ground and dies, it remains only a single grain'

(John 10:24). We want love without any dyings. We want to find life without losing it. We would prefer happiness minus the Beatitudes, good news minus grit. Most of all we want the illusion of not being down-and-out, and so we miss the truth that sets us free – that we can meet God most in our down-and-out-ness.

To see only a serene and peace-giving Jesus is to miss the conflict in the gospel story; it is to suppress the strand that culminates in his murder. But conflict was there from the outset, even in the Annunciation. Thousands of paintings have portrayed that scene as bathed in golden light; they seldom capture what is so strongly expressed in the text, that at first Mary was 'deeply disturbed' by the angel's message and that it was a long road of anxious questioning before her surrender of 'let what you have said be done to me' (Luke 1:38).

I have known this pattern so often in my own life and in others – the road that leads through struggle to new simplicity. I recall a woman on a retreat who discovered that she was manageress of all she surveyed, including God; it was tough but liberating to learn another language of life. Or I think of a good friend in hospital after a breakdown, and of his humbled but hopeful laughter over a notice there: 'The management regrets any inconvenience caused during reconstruction.' Letting go of habits of control is frightening at first, but it is a crucial moment on any road towards faith. To enter into one's poverty brings a language of reverence before reality and before God. The full range of our humanity is like a skyscraper with many storeys, some of them neglected or unvisited. Reverence born from meeting fragility is one of them. The conflict of this tenth step comes from avoiding the pain of experiencing our deep frailty. But to risk that encounter can open long-locked doors into the possibility of faith.

In this light a remarkable scene comes early on in Mark's gospel (chapter 3), that brings together both healing and conflict, the Jesus of tenderness and the Jesus who shocks. The scene shows him having to face conflict within the synagogue. Before he 'enters' symbolically into this sacred place, a contrast awaits him in the shape of a man with a withered hand and the watching religious establishment. Thus from the outset there is stark opposition between crying need and cold suspicion, between oppressed and oppressor. The word that echoes menacingly through the story is 'they' – a group left anonymous until the end. 'They' are there to trap Jesus, to fuel their accusations about him as a law-breaker.

He had always sided with the wounded ones; now it leads him into trouble with the ruling elite. He calls the handicapped man forward, to stand there as a summary of human suffering, and facing 'them' with this picture of need, he poses his fundamental question. 'Is it against the law on the sabbath to save life?' The drama intensifies as 'they' remain silent. Although the official keepers of God's word, they have lost God's answer to this question. They have distorted the first love because they are not living the second. Their compassion has dried up; they have opted for sacrifices rather than mercy; and so the God of Revelation has become, in their system, a god of oppressive laws and external rituals.

Their very silence is an answer to his question, a sign of their inability to give life. They have joined the destroyers. And 'he looked around at them with anger' because their 'hearts' were imprisoned in a coldness beyond him – God's frozen people! Every time the gospels speak of the anger of Jesus it is connected with the ravages of religion at its worst – in a money-making temple or faced later with the dehumanizing power structures of the Pharisees. This synagogue scene reaches its climax when Jesus speaks into a double silence: against their closed silence, he turns to the silent man of suffering. 'Stretch out your hand'. And it was healed. But 'immediately' they depart planning to 'destroy' him. His love story proved too disturbing for the settled ones.

So there is no escaping the vehemence of Christ in the gospels. Why such an uncomfortable tone in the person who is meant to embody love? The answer is quite simple: love *is* uncomfortable, but we would prefer it not to be. Jesus saw through that softer option, in the course of his struggle in the desert between two languages of life. One was the way of showy power; the other was the way of trusting poverty. That desert discovery later gave edge to his judgements of others, his vehemence being often provoked by seeing people in danger of missing his own insight – the basic happiness of being 'poor in spirit'. The vehemence of Jesus is that people should be free, and it has its roots in love and in anger: love because he sees the possibilities in everyone, and anger because he sees them trapped in power-games and falsities, and avoiding their down-and-out-ness. If they stay there, if they do not learn to measure life differently, they will lack the freedom for faith.

GOSPEL SHOCK IN FICTION

Redemption is meaningless unless there is a cause for it . . . You have to make your vision apparent by shock – to the hard of hearing you shout, and for the almost-blind you draw large and startling figures. Flannery O'Connor

Rather than any scripture scholar or theologian, the fiction of Flannery O'Connor has helped me to understand this more vehement side of Christ. She died in her late thirties in 1964 and her reputation has grown ever since as one of the best short-story artists of the century and, among creative writers, as uniquely alert to theological issues. (One of her letters describes with humour how she would always read Aquinas for twenty minutes before going to bed.) As the quotation above suggests, her focus was on the unrecognized need for redemption in people today. More particularly she loved to mock the many faces of pride, seeing them as evasions of what she called 'existential' poverty. 'Everybody', she wrote in one of her letters, 'is The Poor'. The vehemence of her stories was directed against forgetting this poverty and her strategy was twofold: to bring a character into painful contact with his or her pride and poverty, and then to go further into an 'action of grace'.

My favourite example of this can be captured in one sentence from the end of 'A Good Man is Hard to Find' (even the title is tongue-in-cheek). But obviously we need the context to appreciate it. The main character in the story is 'the grandmother', someone who always gets her way and who manages on this occasion to persuade a family outing to take a wrong turning (literally) in search of an old house she once knew. But down this 'dirt road' they fall into the clutches of a notorious bandit, called 'the Misfit'. The grandmother remains confident that she can talk her way out of the crisis, even while the others with her are being shot in the woods by one of the Misfit's men. She keeps telling him that he is a 'good man' and she talks to him about Jesus and prayer. At one point the Misfit remarks that he does not know whether Jesus raised the dead, and this leads to the climax of the story:

> 'Listen lady,' he said in a high voice, 'if I had of been there I would of known and I wouldn't be like I am now.' His voice seemed about to crack and the grandmother's head cleared for an instant. She saw the man's face twisted close to her own as if he were going to cry and she murmured. 'Why you're one of my babies. You're one of my own children!' She reached out and touched him on the shoulder. The Misfit sprang back as if a snake had bitten him and shot her three times through the chest. Then he put his gun down and took off his glasses and began to clean them . . . 'She would of been a good woman,' the Misfit said, 'if it had been somebody there to shoot her every minute of her life.'

That last sentence is a beautifully off-beat summary of Flannery O'Connor's vision. Only as she faces death, does the grandmother stumble out of her pride into a moment of compassion. 'For an instant' she is shocked into being a 'good woman': when at last she is weak, then is she strangely strong. This is exactly what Christ was doing in his more vehement moments – trying to jolt people out of their pride and into an honest hunger.

In one of her essays Flannery O'Connor commented that 'the basic experience of everyone is the experience of human limitation'. Her stories are about the dangerous ways in which people run from that reality, and create self-systems impregnable to change – until disturbing grace arrives. The human security system is the target of her comedy and the reason for what she called her 'violent literary means'; she highlights our poverty-denying pride, and the extent to which it can block faith.

One of the many books written about her work is entitled *The Pruning Word*, which is of course a gospel image about the life of faith – the pruning of the vine that it may bear more fruit. In her view our world is closed against the need for God, and in particular against any need for the freedom that is called salvation. As she puts it, where our 'sense of evil is diluted or lacking', we will avoid 'the price of restoration'. Therefore she sets out to shatter this smugness both in her characters and in her readers. Her approach is comic and ironic (like many of the parables of Jesus), but her purpose is deadly serious: it is a reminder of the cost of faith. Her stories entail a facing of self-poverty and a pruning of pride, and only then an awakening to forgotten possibilities.

Throughout her writings I find a wisdom that helps me to understand the pruning side of the gospel. In the vehemence of her stories I glimpse something of gospel shock and a unity of attitude in Christ. From the rougher scene of his throwing the traders out of the temple to the gentler toughness with which he challenges the rich young man, he is acting out of the same basis: a love that wants people to be free for love. That is the point of all the pruning – to face our down-and-out-ness and so be ready to receive the flow of the down and out loves.

SCAFFOLDING FOR REFLECTION

Our first step dealt with disposition, and likewise our last. Here we have been exploring the resistance to what is traditionally called 'humility'. Who do I think I am? Who do I think God is? Until I face my own poverty honestly, I will not be ready for faith. Until I learn reverence for a wisdom beyond me, I will never be free for the strange ways of God.

What is offered here falls into two parts. The first looks at a section of Scripture where letting go of normal values is stressed in a particular way. Then we shall have some modern texts on this theme.

Here the task for the reader is to identify in personal terms where the poverty of powerlessness has been experienced and to become aware of the crisis and conflict of attitudes within one's own life.

In three central chapters of Mark's gospel, Jesus speaks three times about the way he is going to die, and on each occasion he runs into resistance from his close followers. First, it is Peter who questions the need for suffering and, in words that echo the struggle of the desert, is told: 'Get behind me, Satan! Because the way you think is not God's way but man's' (Mark 8:33). Later, the whole group of disciples were arguing over precedence among themselves; so he tells them that the first must be 'servant of all' and takes a child in his arms as another way of reversing their values (Mark 9:36). The third occasion involves the ambitious brothers, James and John, who wanted to book the principal seats with Christ in his kingdom; to them he speaks of sharing his 'cup' and his 'baptism' of death, and again he challenges them with his different view of authority, where the greatest will be the 'servant' (Mark 10:39–44).

There can be no mistaking the struggle of attitudes at stake here, or the fact that Christian faith entails an overturning of what is assumed to be common sense and realistic and natural.

In that same tenth chapter of Mark comes the episode with the man who is looking for life but unable to let go of his possessions. He is a good man in the sense that he has been living the life of the commandments. But he remains unfree. The pivotal sentence tells us that Jesus 'looked steadily at him and loved him', and it is crucial that this comes before offering the larger challenge, 'there is one thing you lack' (Mark 10:21). It would be possible to take this text as a spring-board for personal meditation – of the ways in which Christ loves each one and yet has huge hopes for liberating us from our cramping securities. It could also be approached as an image of our late-twentieth-century culture – with its mixture of good-will and unfreedom, and its being blocked from faith by being confused by a sensate and successful world of technology.

The contemporary German theologian Johannes Baptist Metz published a little booklet nearly twenty years ago that I know to have been of immense help to many people. Entitled *Poverty of Spirit* it explored some of the issues at the heart of Step Ten here. In Metz's view humanity is confronted with a fundamental choice, either to accept one's innate poverty or to become the slave of anxiety:

A man with grace is a man who has been emptied, who stands impoverished before God, who has nothing of which he can boast . . .

It is the doorway through which men must pass to become authentic human beings. Only through poverty of spirit do men draw near to God; only through it does God draw near to man . . .

All the great experiences of life – freedom, encounter, love, death – are worked out in the silent turbulence of an impoverished spirit. A gentleness comes over man when he confronts such decisive moments. He is quietly but deeply moved by a mature encounter; he becomes suddenly humble when he is overtaken by love. A certain lustre plays over the visage of a dying man. As a man draws near to his real wellsprings, his thoughts become devout, his understanding mellows, and his words slacken. His judgement becomes reserved and his objectivity becomes reverent . . . The reason is that in such experiences the moment of truth arrives.

More recently the same theme has been lucidly expressed by Laurence Freeman in *Light Within:*

Poverty of spirit is an essential human experience to pass through. If we don't pass through it, we don't break into reality . . . We call it *poverty* only because material poverty is a metaphor for us to understand this spiritual condition. It is called poverty because poverty is a state where we have touched rock-bottom . . .

We resist this poverty instinctively and a kind of gravitational force pulls us away from it because we prefer the illusion of ourselves as being independent of our Creator. In that false light of independent status we develop the Luciferian, egotistical notion of having a *relationship* with God as a relationship of equals. We lose the humble realism of understanding that because of his utter generosity we have *communion* with him, which is something much greater than relationship.

Something of the same wisdom can be found in less religious language in an exciting book by the Brazilian, Roberto Mangabeira Unger, who is professor of law and

social theory at Harvard. Entitled *Passion: an Essay on Personality*, it looks on the 'entire form of social life' as having the
'quality of a prison'. In this perspective he speaks of faith (as
well as hope and love) as a transforming passion which our
world needs to counter the habits of domination and self-
interest. He comes closest to our concerns of this tenth step
in his emphasis that faith stems from some experience of
vulnerability. So we end this section with Unger's eloquent
words about emerging from prisons into the new freedom of
faith:

> The cycle of hatred, vanity, jealousy, and envy increasingly
> constricts the realm of human freedom until the cycle is
> broken by a force external to itself. The career of faith,
> hope, and love, however, may decisively enlarge the area of
> social life in which human reconciliation can take hold . . .
>
> Love exists when you experience the existence of the
> other person as a confirmation of your own . . . Faith, like
> hope, occupies a place of its own within the larger economy
> of love. Even if we give a purely secular interpretation to
> faith, we can distinguish two elements in it. The first and
> most basic of these is the willingness to open yourself up
> to another person or to place yourself in his hands. The
> second element is the more familiar, cognitive jump:
> characteristically, you do not know how to justify the
> hazard of personal openness and vulnerability. If someone
> challenged you to show that you were justified in under-
> taking the risk, you could not do so.

Epilogue

Each day forces us
to totter on planks we hope
will become bridges.
          A haiku by Kevin Hart

A REALITY CHECK

An Eastern parable tells of a man on his knees in the grounds
of the temple, searching for a lost key. A friend comes to help
him and asks, 'Where were you when you think you lost it?'
'At home,' comes the surprising reply. 'Then why waste time
looking for it here?' 'Because the light is better here.'

For my part I think I was many years in religious life
before I accepted that I encounter God through reality. I
kept looking in the holy places. There seemed to be more
light there. But I have come slowly to the conviction that the
whole of life is the call of God and that life is not lived in
chapel corners.

I have many friends who will never share my Christian
faith. Still I hope this book will have meant something to
them, that it will not be too far from their experiences – of
struggling to be free, of searching to make sense, and of
standing with pained puzzlement before the mystery of things.
For me the Revelation of God in Jesus is the truth about
reality. My unbelieving friends cannot say 'yes' to that vision,
but they can say another 'yes' which in some ways is even
more important – a 'yes' to loving in reality. In the night-
time encounter of Jesus with Nicodemus there is the saying:
'He who does the truth comes out into the light' (John 3:21).

Yes, it is through living with love that the light becomes visible. Yes, faith is secondary to love.

A SLOW ROAD

One of the most famous of scriptural stories (Luke 24) tells of a journey from disillusionment into joy, and it is told, like all good stories, as an unfolding of stages.

The story starts with two friends walking away from faith, or so they think. They ponder the past, stunned by the collapse of their hopes.

But they are not alone; a Stranger walks with them, asking to hear their story.

When he has heard them out, he does not reject their experience but challenges their interpretation. He has other lights to read it by.

(Later they will look back and find that their hearts seemed to burn as they listened to him: they were escaping from the small self disappointed over false hopes, and beginning to quest with the Stranger for the larger meaning of it all, especially of suffering.)

When he seems to be taking another road, they come to a threshold of choice; in a moment of crucial freedom they invite the Stranger home.

All those steps have found echo in the pages of this book, but not the final two moments: the symbolic encounter in the breaking of bread, and the return to the community, carrying news of resurrection.

Today there is not so much a crisis of faith as a crisis of living symbols and a dearth of community. Where faith is flourishing, it will be found rich in symbols and rich in community. A book cannot take the place of such symbolic encounters. Reading is an isolated business but it can point towards community. It is enough if it clears the ground a little, and makes more possible that finding of the Stranger, who can give hope for love.

BY WAY OF SUMMARY

Struggles to escape are lifelong, unstable and like the old down-slides in 'snakes and ladders', we can often bump back to zero.

The quest for truth is perennial, ever changing, never done. To talk about it is easy. To live it is more exciting and more expensive.

Love stories surround us as gradual gifts of the Spirit, for each day and for eternity – a love that seeks out those who seem at zero.

Quick Review of the Ten Steps

Getting Free

THE FIRST ESCAPE
from a false self, imprisoned in negative attitudes, to a true self, generous and alive; this means patience with the shadows, until able to be still and in touch with deeper feelings.

THE SECOND ESCAPE
from the pressures of a superficial context to the courage to live differently: more simply, more contemplatively, and finding some alternative community for support.

THE THIRD ESCAPE
from thinking about God in 'out there' language to the wonder that can reverence Mystery and ask genuine questions about religious truth.

THE FOURTH ESCAPE
from the unworthy and immature gods of childhood images to the human face of God revealed in Christ.

Finding Focus

THE FIRST QUEST
the heart that follows its hungers, staying with its restlessness, waiting until the time is ripe to say 'yes'.

THE SECOND QUEST
the mind that seeks for meaning, wrestling with the many 'why?'s of existence.

THE THIRD QUEST
the conscience, awake to self-deceptions and to the scandals of our divided world, yet struggling to discover what is right and best.

THE FOURTH QUEST
the inner spirit that does not run from silence, that experiences something of its own depths, and learns there to listen for God's word.

Love Where Faith is Born

THE FIRST LOVE STORY
finding that God draws near, in Jesus Christ, encountering him personally, being surprised by his understanding and the power of his compassion.

THE SECOND LOVE STORY
humbled into honesty by the unsteadiness of one's loving, shocked by the challenges of the gospel, one becomes more ready to let go of self and of one's resistances to faith.

Main Authors Cited

Arias, Juan, *The God I Don't Believe In*, trans. P. Barrett. Mercier, Dublin, 1973.

Balthasar, Hans Urs von, *Elucidations*. SPCK, London, 1975.

—, *Engagement With God*, trans. G. Halliburton. SPCK, London, 1975.

—, *The Glory of the Lord*, vol. I, trans. E. Leiva-Merikakis. Clark, Edinburgh, 1982.

Duffy, Eamon, 'Encountering God: when belief fails' in *Encounters: Exploring Christian Faith*, ed. M. Mayne. DLT, London 1986.

Ellul, Jacques, *The Ethics of Freedom*, trans. G. Bromley. Eerdsmans, Grand Rapids, 1976.

—, *The Presence of the Kingdom*, trans. O. Wyon. Seabury, N.Y., 1967.

—, *The Technological Society*, trans. G. Wilkinson. Vintage Books, N.Y., 1964.

Hodges, H. A., *God beyond Knowledge*, ed. W. D. Hudson. Macmillan, London, 1979.

Kavanaugh, John Francis, 'Capitalist Culture and Christian Faith', *The Way* 25 (1985).

—, *Following Christ in a Consumer Society*. Orbis Books, N.Y., 1981.

Kroner, Richard, *The Religious Function of Imagination*, Yale, New Haven, 1941.

Lonergan, Bernard, *Method in Theology*. DLT, London, 1972.

—, *A Second Collection*. DLT, London, 1974.

—, *A Third Collection*, ed. F. Crowe. Geoffrey Chapman, London, 1985.

Lubac, Henri de, *The Discovery of God*, trans. A. Dru. DLT, London, 1960.

Lynch, William, *The Image Industries*. Sheed & Ward, London, 1960.

Metz, Johannes B., *Poverty of Spirit*, trans. J. Drury. Paulist Press, N.Y., 1968.

Montefiore, Hugh, *The Probability of God*, SCM Press, London, 1985.

O'Connor, Flannery, *A Good Man is Hard to Find and Other Stories*. Women's Press, London, 1980.

—, *Mystery and Manners. Occasional Prose*, ed. S. Fitzgerald. Faber & Faber, London, 1972.

Rahner, Karl, 'Experience of Self and Experience of God', *Theological Investigations* XIII. DLT, 1978.

—, *Foundations of Christian Faith*. Seabury Press, N.Y., 1978.

Schumacher, E. F. *A Guide for the Perplexed*. Sphere Books, London 1978.

Teresa of Jesus, The Life of, trans. E. Allison Peers. Image Books, Doubleday, N.Y., 1960.

Unger, Roberto Mangabeira, *Passion: an Essay on Personality*. Collier Macmillan, London, 1984.